Sta. Clara Co. Library
CENTRAL REFERENCE   OCT 3 0 '90

P9-BJK-869

Santa Clara County Free Library

REFERENCE

5816

Inventors
and Their
Inventions

INVENTORS AND THEIR
INVENTIONS : A
CALIFORNIA LEGACY SEEN
THROUGH THE EYES OF A
PATENT ATTORNEY
33305001024318

Inventors
and Their
Inventions

A California legacy

seen through the eyes

of patent attorney

Paul D. Flehr

PACIFIC BOOKS
Palo Alto, California

SANTA CLARA COUNTY LIBRARY

• 3 3305 00102 4318

Copyright © 1990 Paul D. Flehr.

All rights reserved. No part of this book may be reproduced,
stored in a retrieval system, or transmitted in any form or
by any means, electronic, mechanical, photocopying, recording,
or otherwise without the prior written permission of the
copyright holder, excepting brief quotes used in connection
with reviews written specifically for inclusion in a magazine
or newspaper.

Library of Congress Cataloging-in-Publication Data

Flehr, Paul D., 1898–
    Inventors and their Inventions: a California legacy seen
    through the eyes of patent attorney / Paul D. Flehr.
       p.   cm.
    ISBN 0-87015-261-0
     1. Inventors–California.   2. Inventions–California.
    3. Patent laws and legislation–California.   I. Title.
    T22.C2F54   1989
    608.7794–dc20   89-71123
                                                      CIP

Book and jacket design, and composition by Reprographex.
Printed and bound in the United States of America.

Pacific Books, Publishers
P.O. Box 558
Palo Alto, California 94302-0558, U.S.A.

Foreword

THIS BOOK HAS BEEN TAKING SHAPE THROUGH A LONG AND RICH lifetime of experience in the field of intellectual law. Paul D. Flehr, the author, has been mentor, adviser, and inspiration to many attorneys, including the undersigned. It is a true pleasure to contribute this foreword as a small token of acknowledgment for the invaluable benefits of long association with a man who deserves our respect and admiration.

Paul was born in Ironton, Ohio in December 1898, of parents of German ancestry. As a teenager he became interested in "wireless"—de Forest's detector tubes, rotary spark transmitters, and the like. He was soon building and selling his own wireless equipment in Ironton. In 1917, Paul entered Ohio State University to study electrical engineering. The U.S. Navy tapped him as a future submarine officer, and accordingly his major field of study was switched to mechanical engineering. Fortunately the war ended while Paul was in training, and he was able to continue his education and graduate in 1921. Soon thereafter he took a position in Washington with the U.S. Patent Office as an examiner concentrating on the burgeoning radio industry. During that time, he also attended George Washington University and received his law degree within three years.

In 1925, Paul moved to San Francisco and joined the patent law firm of White, Prost, and Evans, the predecessor of which had been founded in 1912. He later became a partner in that firm and some successor firms. In 1934 he established an independent practice in San Francisco. John Swain joined him in 1942, and in 1947 they formed the partnership firm of Flehr and Swain. We both joined that firm in 1952, after graduating from the University of California's Law School in Berkeley. After Swain's death in 1963, the firm name was changed to Flehr, Hohbach, Test, Albritton, and Herbert, in October 1966.

Our firm has grown over the years to approximately thirty attorneys, but Paul Flehr has always been our wise and thoughtful leader. At the age of 90, he continues to be a daily presence in the firm, still practicing law and offering guidance and advice to all. Throughout the years, Paul has always maintained a strong interest in his work. He has taken great effort to be sure every new attorney entering the firm received the best possible training. He has never been too busy to help. His personal interests have always been subservient to the needs of the firm and its clients. We and all the partners and associates of the firm will always be deeply indebted to Paul for his unselfish leadership.

Paul has often expressed his feeling that too many inventors are virtually unknown and fail to receive the recognition they deserve. Paul has finally made the time to gather in this book his recollections about some of the fascinating patent situations he has dealt with over the years in the San Francisco area, and particularly what came to be known worldwide as Silicon Valley. We are certain Paul shares our hope that the readers of this book will enjoy some of the enthusiasm he has shown over his years of working with these inventors and their inventions.

Harold C. Hohbach   Aldo J. Test

September 6, 1989

Preface

OUR WORLD IS CONSTANTLY BEING CHANGED BY INVENTORS AND THEIR inventions. Why? Many reasons have come to mind as I prepared this book. Some inventors have a strong creative urge and simply love the feeling of creative accomplishment. Others have a desire to produce new things or new methods that will have a positive impact on society or history—medical advances, for example. There are inventors in industry whose job is to keep up with, or surpass, the competition. Some see a successful invention as adding to their personal prestige or financial status. In recent years we have seen significant inventions emerge from research departments of our major universities, such as Stanford and the University of California. Their contributions in medical and agricultural fields have been of particular importance.

Today many inventors are employees of large companies or corporations. Typically, their work results in improvements to the organization's products or processes, or in new things that their employers want to commercialize. If the organization is large enough, it may have a research and development department organized into groups, each with a project leader. Smaller companies may deal with inventions less formally; the inventor may be an engineer or technician engaged in the manufacturing operations. Inventors employed by an organization are generally required to assign their inventions to the employer, but if the item is successfully commercialized, the inventor may still benefit substantially—with increased prestige or salary. Relatively few inventors have the ability or drive to take on the task of commercializing their own inventions and developing their own companies; their minds work in other directions.

I have observed a close relationship between the economy of an area and its inventions. A region with a poor economy has few inventors, or in any case few worthwhile inventions are made there. In contrast, if the economy of an area is healthy, there is general optimism and growth, and inventors and their inventions go along with the regional trend. California has had a growing economy ever since it became a state in 1850. Today it has more inventors per capita than any other state of the country. Many California corporations and companies have substantial research and development groups. Our major universities engage in research in a wide variety of fields. And we still have a good number of independent inventors.

The various stories told in this book relate events that I personally recall from my long practice as an attorney in the field of "intellectual law," which includes patents, trademarks, copyrights, and trade secrets. These are the stories of certain California inventors that I have known—how their inventions were made, and their experiences in commercializing and marketing those inventions. Some of them built sizable corporations on the basis of their inventive work and the patents obtained for them.

I first came to the San Francisco area in 1925 and have practiced here continuously since then. At that time, there was little important manufacturing industry here, although there were many small firms making specialized products. Buy-outs of these local companies by larger eastern firms were common, and many times the purchasing group transferred local operations to their existing eastern establishments. Today, while we still have buy-outs and mergers, the local operations are more often maintained or even enlarged, as the eastern interests have a better recognition of California's economic strength and importance.

Many of the large corporations in the San Francisco area were based on local inventions and the resulting patent rights. Some organizations owe their present existence to courageous inventors who carried on through hard times. The stories in this book are those of such creative and persistent people.

Paul D. Flehr
May 18, 1989

Contents

Charles W. Merrill
Gold Recovery from Cyanide Solutions

Merrill's early experiences as a graduate mining engineer featured development of a process and equipment for removing gold from cyanide solutions. He organized a company in San Francisco to license his process and sell equipment throughout the world.

Sven J. Nordstrom
Pressure Lubricated Valve

This inventor's plug valve was successfully commercialized by Merco Nordstrom Valve Company, financed by Charles W. Merrill, and later acquired by Rockwell Industries.

David D. Peebles
Instant Dry Milk Powder

One of the most prolific inventors in the dairy industry, Peebles was without a formal technical education and had early ambitions as an operatic singer.

Alexander M. Poniatoff
Magnetic Tape Recorder

After many exciting experiences during the period of World War I until he arrived in California, about 1927, he became one of the original organizers of Ampex, where he took the lead in research and development. He maintained an intimate relationship with the invention and development of the video tape recorder.

Walter T. Selsted
Tape Recorders and Consulting

Selsted's technical experiences led him to work as an independent electronics engineer. He was employed by Ampex and Hewlett-Packard and has served as a technical consultant to various other companies and as a technical expert in court actions.

Richard G. Sweet
High-Speed Jet Printer

Sweet's invention was made during government-financed research at Stanford University, and its principles have proved valuable in other forms of related equipment.

Albert R. Thompson
Food Processing Machinery

A prolific inventor without much formal education, Thompson worked for most of his career for only one employer (FMC). He is credited with some two hundred U.S. Patents.

Russell H. Varian
Klystron Tube

Russell Varian is noted for his invention of the Klystron tube, which is known throughout the world and is widely used in microwave communication systems.

William K. Warnock and Frank G. Hubener
Permanent Pressed Garment Process

The term "permanent pressed" refers to garments that keep a pressed appearance after washing and drying. The first commercial use of the process was by Levi Strauss with their jeans. Eventually the patent rights were the subject of lengthy litigation.

Index of Names

Inventors
and Their
Inventions

Felix Bloch and William W. Hansen

Nuclear Magnetic Resonance

Felix Bloch

William W. Hansen

VERY FEW PERSONS CAN BE classed as true scientists, dedicated to making basic scientific discoveries and imparting their discoveries and theories to other scientists. Their discoveries may add to the sum total of our scientific information or they may bring about radical changes in basic scientific concepts. In many instances they make possible new commercial fields with the creation of new industries.

Dr. Felix Bloch was a true scientist who, together with a brilliant electrical engineer, William W. Hansen, invented a method and equipment for demonstrating a basic phenomenon in molecular physics. Bloch was a commanding personality, tall and solidly built, and a positive speaker. He was understanding but unyielding when he considered that his rights were not being observed.

It was my pleasure and honor to serve as Bloch's personal attorney on patent matters over a period that started in 1959 and continued until his death in 1983. For several years before his death he had spent summer vacations in Switzerland and Israel, giving lectures in advanced physics.

In a deposition for a litigation matter involving his patents on nuclear magnetic resonance (NMR), Bloch gave the following information about his academic education and experience in physics.

His academic studies began at the Federal Institute of Technology in Zurich, Switzerland. From there he transferred to the University of Leipzig in 1928, where he obtained his Ph.D. degree. He became an assistant professor of physics at the Federal Institute of Technology in Zurich, in 1929, and then had a fellowship in Holland for one year. Following that he became an assistant to Professor W.

K. Heisenberg of the University of Leipzig. He interrupted his stay in Leipzig for about six months to work with Professor Niels Bohr in Copenhagen. Bloch then returned to Leipzig and was again assistant lecturer of that university until the spring of 1933. In the winter of 1933-34 he had a fellowship in Rome with Professor Enrico Fermi. He came to California's Stanford University in 1934.

At one point in his deposition Bloch was requested to describe his conception of NMR. In his technical terminology his reply was as follows:

> My first realization was that the polarization which one had to expect to exist in a constant field, and which, of course, was well known from normal paramagnetism of electrons, that such a polarization would also have to exist because of the magnetic moment of nuclei, and that the phenomenon of magnetic resonance would also have to occur in bulk matter. The principal question was how one could actually measure its occurrence.
>
> At that point it occurred to me that if one can cause a precession of the nuclear polarization by magnetic resonance in bulk matter one would deal with alternating components of the polarization perpendicular to the DC field, and that this fact ought to exhibit the well-known features of electromagnetic induction according to Faraday's law of induction.
>
> Thus, what was required was a coil in which this induced voltage would be developed, and at a later stage detected.
>
> I believe, Mr. Anderegg [opposing counsel], if you want to have the actual basic fact of my discovery, I would like to formulate it to say that it consists in the observation of electromagnetic effects due to the change of orientation of magnetic moments in bulk matter.

To anyone except a scientist versed in physics the above is virtually incomprehensible; even the specification of the original patent (2,561,489) is difficult to understand, unless one has a fair knowledge of the structure of molecules and atoms, plus a knowledge of higher mathematics used by scientists.

It appears that Dr. Bloch's co-inventor, Dr. William W. Hansen, did not collaborate with Bloch at the time of the latter's original conception in March 1945, although Hansen was a noteworthy scientist who was known to Bloch at that time.

Unfortunately, Hansen died in the latter part of 1945, shortly before the first successful operation of NMR apparatus on January 4, 1946. However, he worked with Bloch in the design and construction of the apparatus that was used for the first successful operation.

Hansen and Bloch examining early NMR equipment, before the first successful test

In Bloch's preparation for his deposition in a patent infringement action, he said that Hansen visited him in Cambridge, Massachusetts, in May 1945. The two had lunch in Boston and at that time Bloch explained his ideas and asked Hansen's opinion as to whether or not his ideas were practical. He recognized that certain electronic circuitry was required in the building of apparatus to try out the ideas, and that the circuitry would necessarily require great sensitivity to detect the relatively small amount of energy he would have due to precession of nuclei in a magnetic field.

One of the first written documents prepared by Bloch in connection with his ideas was a notebook in which he recorded the mathe-

William Hansen at Stanford Linear Accelerator

matical equations he used to determine the quantitative character of the varying magnetic field that might be expected with the system he was contemplating. One of his concerns was that the amount of energy produced would not be sufficient to activate the response circuitry. He advised Hansen of the amount of energy anticipated by his mathematical analysis. Hansen believed that this amount of energy was sufficient to activate response circuitry, although he indicated that special circuitry would be required. At the conclusion of the luncheon it was understood that Hansen would collaborate in further developing Bloch's ideas, and in transforming them into practice. It was agreed that this further work would be carried out at Stanford University.

Dr. Bloch arrived at Stanford University in Palo Alto, California at the end of July, and Hansen returned to Stanford about the middle of August 1945. They started immediately to plan the nature of the equipment to be constructed, and it was understood that Hansen would supervise the design and construction of the electronic equipment, since he was noted for his work in the electronic field, particularly the design and construction of microwave equipment. Components of the electronic circuitry were purchased from various supply houses in the San Francisco Bay area.

Dr. Martin Packard was a graduate physicist from Oregon State University. He visited Bloch in the middle of September 1945 and at that time a disclosure of the invention was made to him. Because of his interest in the project and the favorable impression he made on Bloch, it was arranged that he would join the project as a research assistant.

Packard joined the project about the end of September 1945 and immediately began checking Hansen's plans for electronic equipment. Packard then proceeded with the ordering and procuring of necessary component parts. As these parts were received, he proceeded to build the equipment.

The project was substantially completed and in condition for testing shortly before Christmas of 1945. The initial tests indicated that the equipment was out of balance, and further adjustments and refinements were made. During the Christmas vacation Bloch

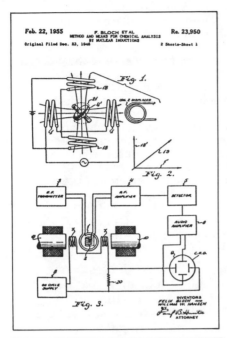

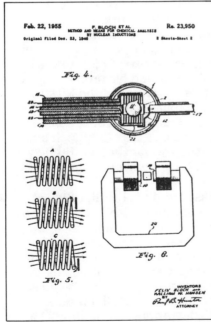

Drawings from Patent Re. 23,950

remained at Stanford doing further work on the magnet part of the project. Packard left for a few days after Christmas. When he returned at the end of December 1945, tests were made on the equipment and the first successful results were seen on January 4, 1946. Packard fixed this date because it was a few days after he had returned from Christmas vacation. Bloch remembers the date because his wife's birthday was on January 3 and he had forgotten to get her a present. When he returned home late in the evening he apologized for not having a birthday present, but told her that her present was the successful test of the equipment. Bloch also noted in his laboratory notebook that the first successful test was made on January 4.

There is usually an element of drama when an invention is successfully tested for the first time, particularly if the objective has never previously been accomplished. Bloch was not prone to drama, but his relating of the occasion, many years later, was itself an emotional experience. The test occurred about 11 p.m., after a long day's work on the apparatus. Someone suggested, "Let's give it a try." The sample was water because of its high concentration of hydrogen. The apparatus was so arranged that a response signal indicating resonance would appear on a cathode ray tube. To everyone's delight, the apparatus functioned as anticipated with a signal display that indicated precession of the hydrogen nuclei and a condition of resonance. One can imagine the impact of this short but successful operation. It was the sudden culmination of his concentration and work for many months that would stand as an advance in basic science.

The specification of the Bloch-Hansen Patent 2,561,489 and its reissue Patent Re. 23,950 refers to the early laboratory tests in the following paragraphs:

The earliest result obtained using the apparatus of Figs. 3 and 4 was concerned with the nuclear induction effect for hydrogen. Hydrogen is a highly satisfactory substance to use for initial investigations because it has the highest gyromagnetic ratio of any atom and a high concentration of hydrogen is present in water and many organic substances. These two facts insure a strong signal with relatively weak magnetic polarizing fields. The first signals were obtained from a sample containing only 1/10 c.c. of water. Samples were later increased to 1 c.c.

One striking demonstration of clear resonance is obtained by raising the steady field slightly above the resonance point and then turning it off. The field in a large magnet dies somewhat gradually when the current is turned off, and the signal may be seen to suddenly appear as the magnetic field passes through the resonant value, or the value for which the axes of the nuclei are precessing at 90° to the magnetic field. Numerous other variations of the method of operation all gave results consistent with the theory. Work also has been done on the heavy hydrogen fluorine, etc., with equally satisfactory results.

Although the first successful test was on January 4, 1946, the application that issued as Patent 2,561,489 was not filed until December 23, 1946. There are several versions of what occurred during this interval of almost one year. Russell Varian related to me that he learned about the work of Dr. Bloch either by reading the letters published in the *Journal of Physics* or by attending a scientific meeting where Bloch spoke of his work. At that time Russell Varian and his brother Sigurd were noted for their invention of the Klystron vacuum tube and probably had previously met and known Bloch. Russell Varian appears to be the first to appreciate that the Bloch and Hansen apparatus and method could be useful as an analytical instrument and that it could be commercialized.

Although Russell and his brother Sigurd at that time were associated with Sperry in the manufacture of Klystron vacuum tubes, they probably had in mind the organization of a California company for the manufacture of Klystrons and other vacuum tubes using the same principles. During the course of Russell Varian's conversations with Bloch after January 4, 1946, he proposed the filing of a patent application covering the apparatus and method developed as of that time, and pointing out its utility as an analytical instrument. Up to that time Bloch had given no thought to patenting his apparatus and method. He was quite content with having demonstrated a phenomenon which up to that time had been only theorized upon. However, he consented to the preparation and filing of the patent application.

Bloch was known as a meticulous scientist

Who actually prepared the application is somewhat of a mystery. The style of the specification is unusual and may have been taken largely from one of Bloch's reports. It relates the work of other scientists who were known to Bloch and Hansen and then describes their own work, including the first successful test in January 1946. The claims of the patent are well prepared, like the work of an experienced patent attorney.

In a deposition, Paul Hunter, who prosecuted the application, states that he did not prepare the application and that it was his understanding that the application was prepared by the applicants. Obviously this was in error because Hansen died in 1945 and his brother, who was the sole heir of his estate, was not an engineer. Bloch stated in his deposition, taken about the same time, that he did not prepare the application and did not know who did.

During 1952 I had occasion to contact Russell Varian about various matters. By that time Russell and his brother had organized the corporation now known as Varian Associates, with a manufacturing plant in Redwood City, California. Myrl Stern was then president and Russell Varian was vice president. Russell told me about his early contacts with Dr. Bloch and his preparation of the patent application. This seems logical considering that Russell was the only one involved who had had experience in patent matters and also had the scientific knowledge to understand and appreciate the invention.

Bloch carefully checking an experimental setup

Felix Bloch was a thorough and meticulous scientist. He considered that his early successful tests opened the door to major research on the properties of nuclei, and to determining various methods of using the apparatus and the analytical work that it made possible. This research involved further tests using nuclei of different atoms and exploring ways of using the apparatus in analytical work. Such work followed the first test on January 6, 1946, and continued for many months thereafter.

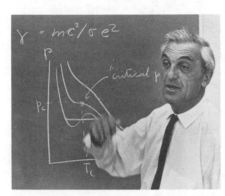

$\gamma = mc^2 / \sigma e^2$

Bloch explaining a theoretical point

The Varian brothers and a group of engineers established a company at an early date to promote their various inventions. The organization was initially a partnership, and later a California corporation. The brothers had access to the work of Bloch and Hansen at Stanford and proceeded to develop a form of NMR apparatus suitable for commercial manufacture and sale. Sometime after the first application was filed in the U.S. Patent Office, Russell Varian negotiated a license agreement with Bloch and the Hansen estate, granting Varian Associates an exclusive license to manufacture and sell the equipment, under the original patent application and further inventions made by Bloch during the course of the agreement. Subsequently, in 1953, the original license was superseded by a second license agreement, which likewise granted exclusive rights to Varian Associates, and was more specific in dealing with possible litigation and with royalty payments. The second license agreement continued until the patent rights expired.

Sometime after filing the original application, Bloch made a further invention which was an improvement to the first apparatus. It was referred to as the spin sample feature of the apparatus. Briefly, it involved spinning the sample at a high speed to obtain improved resolution of the resulting signal. Patents were granted on this feature in the United States (2,960,649) and in several foreign countries. Varian Associates developed a product that could be applied to their standard NMR equipment so that a customer could make use of the spin sample technique whenever it seemed desirable.

As with all inventions that become commercially important, other firms became eager to share in the same business. Instead of relying upon patent infringement actions, Varian adopted the policy of granting sublicenses to established and responsible companies in the United States and foreign countries. Royalty payments continued for the life of the spin sample patent, which expired November 15, 1977.

In 1954 Dr. Bloch became the first director of the European Organization for Nuclear Research in Geneva. In 1974, Bloch was made an emeritus professor of physics at Stanford University. He became Stanford's first Nobel

Bloch with his wife at the Nobel ceremony

laureate and shared the 1952 Nobel Prize in physics for his work on nuclear magnetic resonance. The Nobel award was shared with Edward M. Purcell of Harvard University, who independently constructed and demonstrated comparable apparatus at Harvard.

The NMR patent of Bloch and Hansen is one example of a truly basic invention. Briefly, NMR is the tendency of the core of atoms to vibrate when placed in a strong magnetic field and probed with radio waves. Its basic principles have spread to many industries, including the oil industry, where it found use as an analytical instrument in the development of new products and in making geological surveys. One of the more recent utilizations is as a medical scanner, which may prove to be one of the most valuable tools for developing images of the human body.

Robert E. Clarke

Magnesium Compounds from Sea Water

BEFORE WORLD WAR II, ROBERT E. Clarke was an officer in the United States Army. For a time he was purchasing agent for Anaconda Copper in the Philippine Islands. His personality was impressive and somewhat authoritative. Eventually he became the promoter and driving force of a company known as Marine Magnesium Products Corporation (Marine) located along San Francisco Bay in South San Francisco. I have been unable to determine clearly the parties that originally organized the company, but Clarke very probably was one of the founders, and as president he carried the company through its major ups and downs.

Clarke, together with several engineers employed by the company, also was an inventor of several of the company's processes. This chapter relates the evolution of a practical process for the manufacture of various magnesium compounds by the precipitation of magnesium hydroxide from sea water.

Clarke became involved with Marine in 1931. The company was organized for recovering magnesium hydroxide from sea water, making use of a process developed and patented by Edward K. Judd. A number of men of substantial means were financially involved and became members of Marine's Board of Directors. Clarke became the first president and continued in that capacity until the company was acquired by Merck in 1951. The company obtained an exclusive patent license from Judd under his Patent 1,505,202. Judd was to receive a royalty based upon the sales of magnesium products produced by his process.

The process of precipitating magnesium hydroxide from sea water was well known before Judd's invention, but it had not been commercialized to any extent. For pharmaceutical purposes, where purity is crucial, the Phillips Company precipitated magnesium

Robert E. Clarke

Massachusetts to handle the project and never completed his college work for an engineering degree.

The prototype built according to Abner's ideas apparently worked well and plans were made to produce it commercially in Detroit. For reasons that are not clear, the Detroit enterprise was never carried to the commercial phase and eventually was terminated. Abner then returned to California to join the other members of his family, and convinced them to embark upon the enterprise of developing his steam car. An organization was established, named Doble Laboratories, Inc., and was incorporated in the State of California.

The Doble car had a sporty appearance

Abner was an impressive figure and a convincing talker. He had a prototype steam car, presumably the one made for the Detroit project. Realizing the financial requirements for the commercial manufacture and sale of steam cars, he undertook to raise capital by the sale of shares in the company in San Francisco and the other larger cities of California. Abner had obtained permission from the California Corporation Commissioner to sell a specified number of shares of stock in the company. After selling the prescribed number of shares Abner found that he did not have sufficient capital to proceed with the company, and the Corporation Commissioner refused his application for permission to sell additional shares. Someone, probably Abner, had the idea of selling further stock to Oregon residents, on the theory that this would be outside the jurisdiction of the California Corporation Commissioner. This precipitated a legal action by the Corporation Commissioner that put a stop to such sales, and imposed a fine against Abner. All of this was unfortunate for the future of the company. Nonetheless, during and following Abner's difficulties, the company was active in making further developments and improvements of the Detroit prototype. By 1924 the company was established in a concrete building in Emeryville, California. There was no production of steam cars there at that time, and the finances of the company were at a low ebb. They had managed, however, to organize a good experimental laboratory and a service shop supervised by Warren Doble, Abner's brother.

Mark Lothrop met Warren sometime during the period 1924-1926. Following graduation from Stanford University, Mark had taken a position as draftsman with a firm of patent attorneys in San Francisco. William White of that firm was the lawyer who had won the patent infringement suit for William Doble against the Pelton Company. Doble Laboratories had become a client of the firm, and the patent application work was delegated to Mark. Due in part to his friendship with Warren Doble, Mark became intensely interested in the steam car development, and particularly in the improvements being worked on by Warren. In time his interest led to placing an order for the building of a steam car to specifications that included all the latest developments. The car was eventually completed and delivered in 1930.

Mark's car was always a center of attraction, particularly when it was being driven by his wife. People of that time were surprised that his wife could drive it, believing that one had to be an engineer to do so! They did not realize that the car did not have a clutch or gearshift transmission and was therefore easier to drive than most of the other cars on the road at that time.

About 1933 the Dobles sold Doble Laboratories to two brothers from the east, George and William (Bill) Besler. Their father

Abner Doble

was then president of Central Railroad of New Jersey. Railroads at that time, of course, relied heavily on steam power. As Mark put it, "The Beslers grew up with steam." It is probable that the Beslers had some experience with the Doble car before coming to California, which led them to make the purchase. Warren Doble seemed to have assumed that after the purchase he would continue to manage the company. However, he soon learned that the company would be under the complete control of the Beslers. Mark Lothrop's reaction to the sell-out was that he might not thereafter have the personal attention of Warren to the servicing of his car. In any event Mark sold his car. Since that time the car has passed through a number of hands with servicing by several mechanics to keep it in running condition. As of this writing, Mark believes the car is in Southern California, still in operable condition.

The Doble car in Berkeley

During the course of his work with the company Warren made a number of improvements. A notable one prevented the so-called "surging" of the steam temperature. In the previous system the burner was automatically extinguished when the steam temperature reached about 900° F. Warren's arrangement went into action when the steam temperature reached about 850° F., introducing a small amount of water into the generator tube of the controlling thermostat, thus temporarily reducing the steam temperature and keeping the burner on, but permitting the burner to be shut off when the steam temperature finally rose to about 900° F.

Firms in a number of foreign countries had also become interested in the Doble development. In New Zealand, A & G Price Proprietary obtained a working Doble license; in England the Sentinel Waggon Works was licensed; and in Germany the firm of A. Borsig, G.M.B.H. was licensed. The president of Borsig and his son Karl came to California to visit the Doble plant. Karl Borsig even worked at the plant for a time to become familiar with the details of the car.

Mark was quite pleased with his Doble steamer. He and his wife used it for both city and highway driving. When the car had been parked for some time, it required only a few minutes to build up the steam pressure for normal operation. Steam pressure during operation was normally maintained at about 1500 psi and at a temperature of about 900° F. On one occasion he took me for a ride on Highway 101 leading from San Francisco to Burlingame, and permitted me to drive the car for a short period. The boiler burner was controlled in such a fashion that the burner would be in operation for a short period of about one minute, after which it would cease to operate until the steam temperature and pressure dropped below a set value. Since the engine was directly geared to the rear wheels, no clutch or gear shift was required. As compared to a conventional internal combustion car, the Doble car seemed to run more smoothly and with no vibration. In going down a steep hill it was Mark's practice to put the engine in reverse, to control the speed, although this practice was not necessarily recommended by the Dobles.

The car used a low-grade gasoline as fuel. For average operation the fuel mileage was about nine miles per gallon. In city traffic or hilly country the mileage would be about five miles per gallon. One characteristic of all steam cars was their consumption of feed water. Mark's car, like other Doble cars, had a condenser system that used a heat exchanger comparable to the radiator of a gasoline car. This system was capable of condensing a portion of the exhaust steam, but not under all normal operating conditions. Particularly where the outside temperature was as high as 100° F., such as in the Sacramento Valley, or in Southern California, the water mileage was relatively poor. Under such conditions water stops were required between gasoline fill-ups.

After the Beslers took over the company, Bill Besler undertook to demonstrate that Doble power plants could be used in place of internal combustion engines as power sources for aircraft. He removed the gasoline engine from his personal airplane and substituted a modified Doble steam plant. On April 17, 1933 Bill Besler made a short flight with his plane, thus demonstrating that steam power could be used for aircraft. Langley's early aircraft experiments also used a steam engine. His failure was probably due to the design of his aircraft, rather than its engine. His engine is now on display in the Smithsonian Institution in Washington, D.C.

The Beslers continued to operate Doble Laboratories after the takeover, but most of the work was for the maintenance and updating of cars in the hands of owners located throughout the United States, and in some foreign countries. All told, about 35 Doble steam cars were built. The public retains a nostalgic interest in steam cars, and they are prized by their owners. They command a high price as antiques. The inventions and refinements of the Dobles are not as well known or appreciated.

Over the period of years following 1914 and ending with the sale of the company, the Dobles were granted nine U.S. patents naming one or more of them as sole or joint inventors. The list includes Patents 1,131,683 issued March 16, 1915; 1,161,460 issued November 29, 1915; 1,259,032 issued March 12, 1918; 1,263,653 issued April 23, 1918; 1,273,466 issued July 23, 1918; 1,273,467 issued July 23, 1918; 1,354,898 issued October 5, 1920; 1,359,041 issued November 16, 1920; 1,359,042 issued November 16, 1920; and 1,359,235 issued November 16, 1920.

Ray Dolby

Noise Reduction in Audio-Recording Systems

WE COMMONLY DESCRIBE successful men as dedicated workers in particular fields and as high achievers. Ray Dolby is certainly all of that. In addition, he has inventive ability in the technical field of audio, plus the demonstrated ability to establish and develop a substantial industrial organization, Dolby Laboratories, which itself is innovative in its commercial methods.

Dolby's name is well known to the public and to engineers interested in sound quality. The trademark "DOLBY" appears on such consumer products as audio amplifiers and cassette tape recorders, and is recognized for high quality, in that the reproduced sound is relatively free of annoying hiss and other noises.

As early as during his high-school years in Redwood City, California, Dolby evidenced interest in electrical and electromechanical devices, electronics, photography, motion-picture techniques, sound equipment, and sound recording. Because of his varied interests, he was put in charge of technical aspects of his high school's audio-visual equipment, which was maintained for classroom use. His work involved keeping the equipment in good operating condition and making any repairs when necessary.

At that time the Ampex Electric Company was in its infancy, with the professional tape recorder, Model 200, its principal product. Alexander Poniatoff, founder and then president of the company, needed a 16mm movie projector for use at a forthcoming meeting of a mental health society in which he was involved. Having learned about the school's equipment, he requested the loan of a projector and was referred to young Ray Dolby. Dolby was impressed with Poniatoff, and

Ray Dolby

undoubtedly Poniatoff was impressed with Dolby, who accompanied Poniatoff to his meeting and showing. During the evening Dolby inquired about the possibility of working for Ampex part-time. Poniatoff explained that there was no opening at that time, but said he would keep Dolby in mind and that he might have use for his services at a later date. Not long after that (summer 1949) Dolby was employed as a technician and assistant to the Ampex development engineers. Dolby's first assignment was to produce calibration tapes for the Ampex Model 200 tape recorder.

Later Dolby assisted in the construction of several specialized recorders, including a multi-track FM tape recorder for the Naval Ordnance Laboratory. During the period 1951-52 he was involved in the development of a tape-recorder-sychronization system, which led to his invention of the all-electronic speed-control system disclosed in Patent 2,797,263. Features disclosed in the patent were later incorporated by Dolby into the Ampex video tape recorder.

Dolby has stated that when he was about twelve or thirteen years of age he became determined to obtain a Ph.D. degree in electrical engineering or physics. In 1951 he started as a freshman at San Jose State College, while continuing to work part-time with Ampex. Beginning in 1952 he started work in connection with the development of the video tape recorder. He graduated from Stanford in 1957 with a B.S. degree in electrical engineering.

As related in the chapter on Charles Ginsburg, during the latter part of 1951 and the early part of 1952 the video tape development project was delegated primarily to Ginsburg and to Dolby. They first agreed upon the general character of the system to be developed, including the use of a rotary head assembly, and then proceeded to build various breadboard models. A working model was completed in November, 1952 and Ginsburg and Dolby gave the first demonstration on November 19, 1952, to Poniatoff and me. A memorandum done at that time by Poniatoff reads as follows:

> To establish a positive record for date when recording of television pictures on

magnetic tape using the Ampex system was reduced to practice, the following notation was made:

(1) On 19 November 1952 the picture was recorded and played back in the presence of the following witnesses:

Charles Ginsburg
Ray Dolby
Paul Flehr
A. M. Poniatoff

(2) The magnetic tape was marked with the date when the recording and playback occurred and was signed by all four witnesses.

(3) The tape is properly packed, labeled, and stored in the Ampex vault, etc.

This tape could be a very important document in case of some future patent court procedures.

Signed
(A. M. Poniatoff)

Ray Dolby has been an inventor since he was a teenager

Again as related in the chapter on Ginsburg, Poniatoff and I questioned Ginsburg and Dolby about the breadboard setup after the demonstration, and they had good answers as to what should be done to improve the system. At the conclusion of the demonstration, which probably took about one half hour, Poniatoff and I returned to his office. In our discussion we agreed that the laboratory setup could be developed into a workable, commercial video tape machine. Poniatoff at that time took occasion to speak about Dolby. He referred to him as "a college boy" with a special knack for putting together circuitry that worked well in particular situations. In other words, I got the impression from him that Dolby was ingenious at devising circuitry to perform various specific functions.

Over the several years required to improve and perfect the video tape recorder, following the demonstration in November, 1952, Dolby was very much involved in making various developments. Dolby's name appears as inventor or co-inventor of a number of inventions covered by patents based on developments made during that period.

The first patent application on the video tape recorder was filed on May 3, 1954 in the joint names of Ginsburg and Dolby. By that time many improvements had been made, and they were incorporated in the patent disclosure. The improvements made in the period 1952-1954 and disclosed in Patent 2,916,546 included Dolby's schemes for switching which made possible unrecorded margins of the tape that were used for recording audio sound and for recording a frequency for the control of the tape speed, a capacitor type of commutating means for the rotary head, photoelectric means forming a part of the head assembly and used as part of the control system, and a four-unit head assembly with the units serially connected in groups of two. Only the amplitude modulation of the video signal was disclosed. The rotary head assembly was arranged to sweep the magnetic units across the tape along arcuate paths.

During further development, after the spring of 1956, it was found that the performance of the unit was handicapped by the poor character of the synchronizing pulses which contained disturbances due to tape dropouts. Dolby initiated development of a processing amplifier that reformed the signal pattern and the synchronizing pulses. The processing amplifier was made the subject of a patent application, which issued as Patent 2,956,114.

Because amplitude modulation was unsatisfactory in certain respects, Dolby, together with other Ampex engineers, developed the present frequency-modulation system. Patent 2,956,114, in the names of Charles P. Ginsburg, Shelby F. Henderson, Jr., Ray M. Dolby, and Charles E. Anderson, discloses this important improvement. This patent was listed by the U.S. Patent Office in a 1976 booklet, distributed in connection with the American Revolution Bicentennial, as an "important" patent.

A more detailed account of Dolby's work with Ginsburg and other Ampex research engineers appears in a preprint of the Society of Motion Picture and Television Engineers, entitled "30th VTR Anniversary—Some Personal Recollections." The presentation was made by Dolby at the 128th SMPTE Technical Conference October 24-29, 1986, in New York.

Dolby had an active part with Ginsburg in the public demonstrations of the video tape machine which took place on April 14, 1956. The Chicago demonstration for the television industry was in Ginsburg's charge and Dolby had charge of the simultaneous demonstration to the press at the Ampex headquarters building in Redwood City, California. Both

Patent filed by Dolby while he was studying in Cambridge, England

demonstrations were dramatically successful and well received by the industry. Ampex received much newspaper publicity and the television stations and networks rushed to place orders for the first production units.

Although Ampex officials were anxious for commercial production at an early date, the machine that was demonstrated was far from being a commercial product. Ginsburg and Dolby tried hard to educate Ampex management about the amount of work and time required before commercial production should begin. The result was a crash program, in which a commercial model was designed, built and tested, with the first units shipped in the fall of 1956. Again Dolby was involved with Ginsburg in making the decisions and changes necessary for commercial production. By this time many other engineers were also involved in the design of the final commercial unit. More detail about these events will be found in the chapters on Ginsburg and Poniatoff.

In June 1957, as mentioned earlier, Dolby graduated from Stanford University with a Bachelor of Science degree in electrical engineering. An award of a Marshall Scholarship, to Cambridge University in England, afforded him an opportunity to study abroad. He entered Pembroke College, Cambridge, in September 1957 and received a Ph.D. degree in physics in December 1961. During his stay in Cambridge he worked in the Cavendish Laboratory from 1957 to 1963, doing research on the properties of long wavelength X rays as applied to electron microprobe analysis. He was elected a Fellow of Pembroke College, Cambridge, in 1961.

From 1963 to 1965 Dolby served as a member of a United Nations advisory team to the Central Scientific Instruments Organization in India. His work in India involved visiting various universities, research organizations, and companies, consulting with their electrical engineering and physics staff. Impressions from these visits were used to shape and create the Central Scientific Instruments Organization, a new Indian government agency in Chandighar, Punjab.

During his stay in India he had time to consider what he would do after his term was completed. Among other things he thought about the possibility of developing apparatus for suppressing or reducing noise in sound-recording equipment. In the development of the processing amplifier for the Ampex video tape machine he had included a crude means for reducing the level of noise pulses of an intensity greater than that of the video signal. He appreciated that it would be worthwhile to develop more sophisticated noise-reduction means for use, for example, in sound-recording studios.

Upon returning to England in 1965 he used his savings to start a small company to which he gave the name Dolby Laboratories. The first establishment was in the corner of a dress-making factory, and the staff comprised three or four people. In 1968 the company moved to its present London location. In 1966 the first customer for the new noise-reduction equipment was the Decca Record Company in London, which had extensive recording studios for making phonograph records. They were interested in reducing the noise level generated by their master tapes. In common with other record companies, it was the practice of Decca to record on master tapes from which the phonograph records were cut. The system that Dolby had in mind would reduce the noise level without degrading the desired recorded sound. By November 1965 Dolby had been able to demonstrate a noise-reduction system, later to be known as the A-type system, which greatly reduced the noise level of the master tapes and made possible the manufacture of phonograph records that consequently had a low noise level.

Decca was pleased with the Dolby noise-reduction system and ordered nine of what was then referred to as the Dolby A301 A-type noise-reduction unit. The first of these units was used in May 1966, to record some Mozart piano concertos played by Vladimir Ashkenazy. The first record actually released by Decca using the Dolby A-type noise-reduction system was Mahler's Second Symphony, conducted by Sir Georg Solti. The record industry and the public soon became acquainted with the quality of these new Decca records and the Dolby system. EMI in England was reluctant to adopt the new Dolby system because of its own work in this field. However, the new system was enthusiastically received by the record industry in the United States, which quickly became aware of the superior quality of records made with the Dolby system.

Dolby at his workbench in 1981

Dolby realized that the consumer field of magnetic tape recorders would be an appropriate market for his noise-reduction concepts. However, the A-type system developed for the recording studios was relatively complicated and expensive, and not suitable for consumer recorders. Beginning in 1967 Dolby developed a simplified noise-reduction system, designated B-type, which was sufficiently inexpensive for use in consumer products. The K.L.H. Research and Development Corporation in Cambridge, Massachusetts encouraged the development of this system and eventually negotiated a license agreement with Dolby. This first license granted by Dolby included the right to use the name "Dolby," which was becoming well known in both the United States and foreign countries. The license granted K.L.H. the right to incorporate the Dolby noise-reduction system in its consumer tape recorders. The first K.L.H. Model 40 tape recorder, using the Dolby B-type system, was introduced to the trade in June 1968. It was well received and greatly enhanced the reputation of the Dolby noise-reduction principles.

The second license granted was to Advent Corporation of Cambridge, Massachusetts. That license covered the production of so-called "black boxes," which were used as a unit added to existing recorders to incorporate the Dolby noise-reduction system. This add-on unit was well received by the trade but eventually it was superseded by cassette recorders incorporating the Dolby B-type noise-reduction system.

In 1968-69 Dolby Laboratories investigated cassette recorders and concluded that, with help, such units might take the place of the open-reel type of recorder for the consumer trade. Dolby undertook to produce a noise-reduction system and further improvements specifically for such machines. In 1969 Dolby demonstrated such an improved compact cassette recorder, with external Dolby B-type noise-reduction, at the Audio Engineering Society Convention in New York. It was well received by the trade as a significant advance in high-fidelity cassette recording.

Dolby traveled to Japan in 1969, 1970, and 1971, to discuss the granting of licenses to several Japanese companies. The first Japanese license was granted to Nakamichi Research, Inc., which specialized in high-fidelity cassette recorders.

Dolby's first license in the United States to K.L.H. specified that the license was exclusive for a limited start-up period. Before granting licenses to Advent and Nakamichi, Dolby gave thought to the development of a standardized form of agreement that would form the basis for a wide licensing program. A new form of license agreement was prepared and used in the licensing of Advent and Nakamichi.

At the summer 1971 Consumer Electronics Show, many cassette recorders with Dolby noise-reduction were shown, all made by Dolby licensees. During the show there was a demonstration to the press and licensees by Dolby Laboratories, of the use of Dolby B-type noise reduction on FM radio. It was also announced at this show that Dolby Laboratories had made an agreement with Signetics Corporation to develop a special integrated circuit for the Dolby B-type noise-reduction system. The integrated circuit widened the range of products in which the Dolby system could be used. Dolby Laboratories also announced details of its new licensing program for consumer products. The new agreement included patent rights, use of Dolby's trademarks, and the use of Dolby's know-how. It covered all consumer audio product categories. Instead of a royalty based on the percentage of sales, it was based on the number of Dolby B-type circuits sold per calendar quarter, the first 10,000 being at $.50 each, the next 40,000 being at $.25, and all above 50,000 being at $.10 each. The royalty rates were tied to the U.S. Consumer Cost of Living Index. For trademark protection and as a service to licensees, Dolby Laboratories established a comprehensive quality-control program.

Announcement of the new license agreements in 1971 resulted in the signing of agreements with nine companies engaged in the manufacture of cassette recorders. Twelve manufacturers were licensed in 1972, and thirteen more in 1973. As of the end of 1986, 160 consumer manufacturers had signed agreements, of which 10 were U.S. licensees and 150 were foreign licensees in 19 different countries.

About 1970 Dolby Laboratories began the development of a sophisticated quality-improvement and noise-reduction system for the motion-picture industry. Initially the movie industry did not appear to be interested but by about 1972 there were indications of real interest. The system was used in "Star Wars" and a number of other successful movies. It employs use of Dolby noise reduction in making the basic sound recording, and also many other signal-improvement technologies in the sound-system-forming parts of the studio-recording and theater-reproducing equipment. The theater part of the system is customized so that it is compatible with the theater's acoustics. The acoustics of each theater may vary according to size, architecture, and construction materials.

Recently Dolby Laboratories has received much publicity about what is termed "surround-sound technology," for theaters, auditoriums, and home use. It involves reproduction of voice, music, and special sound effects in such a manner that side-located loud speakers reproduce stereophonic sounds, a front speaker or speakers may reproduce voice, and an upper speaker located in the ceiling reproduces special sound effects. The object is to provide utmost realism, in conjunction with Dolby noise reduction.

United States Patent [19]

Dolby

[11] 3,846,719

[45] Nov. 5, 1974

[54] NOISE REDUCTION SYSTEMS

[76] Inventor: Ray Milton Dolby, c/o Dolby Laboratories, 590 Wandsworth Rd., London, England

[22] Filed: Sept. 13, 1973

[21] Appl. No.: 397,159

Related U.S. Application Data

[63] Continuation of Ser. No. 173,261, Aug. 19, 1971, abandoned.

[52] U.S. Cl. .... 333/14, 179/1 P, 330/126, 333/17, 333/28 R, 333/70 R, 333/70 CR

[51] Int. Cl. H03g 7/06, H03h 7/10, H04b 1/64

[58] Field of Search .... 333/70 R, 70 CR, 12, 14, 333/17, 18, 28 R; 330/126, 124 R, 151; 328/167-169; 179/100.2 K, 1 D, 1 P

[56]   References Cited
         UNITED STATES PATENTS

2,413,263	12/1946	Suter,	333/70 R X
2,920,281	1/1960	Appert et al.	333/12 X
3,281,723	10/1966	Mercer	333/18

Primary Examiner—James W. Lawrence
Assistant Examiner—Marvin Nussbaum
Attorney, Agent, or Firm—Dike, Bronstein, Roberts, Cushman & Pfund

[57]   ABSTRACT

A noise reduction system comprising a compressor feeding an information channel and a complementary expander treating the output of the channel. The system is applicable to audio and visual signals using compressors and expanders with appropriately scaled frequency selective circuits which narrow the band in which compression and expansion take place as the signal level rises. Distortion and tracking accuracy problems are reduced by the use of compressor and expander configurations embodying a main signal circuit and a further signal circuit, the main circuit providing a first signal which has dynamic range linearity with respect to the input signal and the further circuit providing a second signal which is restricted to a small part of the dynamic range of the signal in the main circuit. The restriction may be effected by one or more variable filter means having a pass band which narrows to exclude large signal components from the compression or expansion action. The second signal is combined additively with the first signal for compressor operation and subtractively for expander operation. True complementarity is attainable by the use of a compressor and expander together to provide an overall noise reduction action without introducing defects into the signal being processed.

71 Claims, 14 Drawing Figures

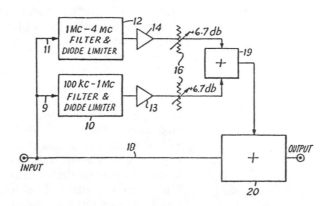

As an indication of the widespread use of the Dolby stereo system, about 5,900 theaters in the United States and over 12,000 more in

Canada and other foreign countries have been equipped with the system.

While preparing this chapter I was invited by Ray Dolby to visit his laboratory at 100 Potrero Avenue, San Francisco. It is a three-story structure built not long after the 1906 San Francisco earthquake. Dolby purchased it in 1980, shortly after establishing his first San Francisco headquarters in a Bank of America building, in the historic Jackson Square area, originally a pickle factory in the 1900 period. He engaged an architectural firm to prepare plans for complete restoration of the 100 Potrero Avenue interior to make it suitable for his operations and to make it artistically attractive as well as functional. At the time of my visit a substantial part of the interior had been renovated but work on some floors was continuing. Much of the new trim was in natural oak. One of the most interesting features under construction was an auditorium with a projection room at one end. The ceiling was beamed with natural oak. The sidewalls were constructed of panels that could be shifted to various positions. Dolby explained that this would make it possible to change the acoustic properties of the auditorium from film screening (requiring dry acoustics) to musical performances (needing more reverberation).

On another floor of the building some circuit boards for noise-reduction systems were being made. The designs of a particular circuit board and its programming were being prepared by research engineers and some boards were partially assembled manually. If they check out properly, additional circuit boards are made by an automatic machine which locates and applies the many small components to the board. The board is then checked by machine to determine if all the components are correctly applied and in their proper positions. Another machine carries out a soldering operation which provides the electrical connections between the components. Finally the completed circuit board is checked out to make certain that it conforms to the design.

One may wonder why this chapter has not included a simple description of the Dolby system. The truth is that there are many Dolby systems designed for different applications, and for new applications that are being developed constantly. During an interview in

1972, Ray Dolby was requested to explain his first system in layman's language. This was his reply:

> I've tried this so many times in so many different ways.... Basically, noise reduction takes place during playback. What we do is have an electronic circuit that detects the presence of any low-level signals or low-level noises. That circuit then feeds its output back to the input and partially cancels out the low-level noises. High-level signals go through untouched.
>
> All previous compressors/expanders had worked on the principle that you have some manipulation of the whole signal. Our techniques sidestep that. We allow the high-level signals to go right through the system—without change. This avoids distortion.

Ray Dolby and Ioan Allen, with the special Oscars they won for their creation of the Dolby Noise Reduction System

Dolby's personality is not one that seeks publicity. However, his accomplishments have made strong impacts on several technical fields as witnessed by many awards and articles appearing in technical literature. His biography in *Who's Who* (British) gives a brief account of his education and early work with Ampex video tape, his subsequent work in India, and the founding of Dolby Laboratories in England and San Francisco. Of his many awards, one of the most interesting was announced by the British Consulate of San Francisco on September 25, 1986 as follows:

> Her Majesty The Queen has awarded an honor to Mr. Ray Dolby of San Francisco, founder and chairman of Dolby Laboratories. He is to become an Officer of the Most Excellent Order of the British Empire (OBE). Since he is an American citizen, the award is honorary. It carries no title.

With respect to his inventions, he is named as inventor or co-inventor in ten U.S. patents relating to the video tape recorder field, and as of August 1987 he has 31 U.S. patents and 13 U.S. pending applications pertaining to his work on noise reduction and related matters.

One should not assume that Dolby's life has been monopolized by his activities in technical fields. He actively pursues hobbies of yachting and skiing. He is a director of the San Francisco Opera Association, Governor of the San Francisco Symphony, and a member of the St. Francis Yacht Club. He is married and has two children.

Federal Telegraph

"The Copper Kettle"

TODAY WE HEAR MUCH ABOUT high-technology electronic companies with the inference that this is a relatively new industrial field. The first electronic company in California, Federal Telegraph Company, was actually started in 1909 and continued until 1931, when it was acquired by International Telegraph and Telephone Company (IT&T) and its operations moved back East. The company was not successful but its activities were noteworthy because of several engineers involved in research and development work there. Some of them became actively associated with new companies in the electronic field and related activities in the years following 1931. These included Leonard F. Fuller, Frederick Kolster, Charles Litton, Paul F. Byrne, and many others.

Federal was organized in 1909 by C. F. Elwell with its corporate offices in San Francisco and its laboratories in Palo Alto. The financial backing came mainly from San Francisco financiers. Augustus Taylor was president in 1925 at the time I first contacted the company. He remained president until the company was acquired by IT&T. Another early corporate officer was Ellery Stone. Leonard Fuller was a vice president in charge of the Palo Alto establishment and a very competent electrical engineer.

About the turn of the century the Philippines became of political and economic importance to the United States. They were independent, friendly and relatively close to Hong Kong and the Asian continent. Rapid communication was important to further the good relationship.

One of the principal purposes of the company was to establish radio telegraph communication between the United States and the Philippine Islands. At that time it was considered impossible to lay a telegraph cable from the United States to the Philippines, as

First building of Federal Telegraph (1909)

had been done across the Atlantic Ocean. They also hoped to establish intercity radio communication between major western cities.

During the period 1909-1918 the radio industry was very much in its infancy. Marconi's system could not reliably transmit messages over great distances, because it did not have a sufficiently powerful radio frequency generator, or a sensitive and reliable receiving detector. One high-power radio frequency generator had been invented by the great Swedish inventor, Valdemar Poulsen. It used an electrical arc operating in a strong magnetic field. Negotiations with Poulsen led to the granting of a license to Federal to commercialize his arc generator. One can only imagine when and where the first Poulsen arc units were manufactured for Federal. Possibly some were made in Sweden. A number of early patents issued to Federal covering improvements to the Poulsen system were in the names of Leonard F. Fuller, Charles V. Logwood, and Cyril F. Elwell.

Original Poulsen arc from Denmark on table, in front of giant Poulsen arc built at Federal Telegraph's Palo Alto plant, 1916-1918. (Left to right: L. F. Fuller, H. F. Elliott, C. C. Chapman, K. Blyer, R. R. Beal, A. L. Anderson)

Shortly after I arrived in California in July, 1925, and became associated with the patent law firm named White, Prost and Evans, I was introduced to the engineering staff of Federal Telegraph in Palo Alto, including Leonard Fuller and Frederick Kolster.

Lee de Forest

THE WHITE HOUSE
WASHINGTON

March 16, 1956

Dear Dr. de Forest:

In this fiftieth anniversary year of a great invention,
I congratulate you on your many contributions to
scientific progress. Through your long and distin-
guished career you must have experienced many
moments of pride that your imagination and talent
furthered the development of modern radio, television and radar. You must also feel great satisfaction in remembering your past decades of service
and in anticipating future achievements that your
handiwork has made possible.

May you enjoy many more years in which to witness
the fruit of your labors.

Sincerely,

Dwight D. Eisenhower

Dr. Lee de Forest
c/o Rear Admiral Ellery W. Stone, USNR
American Cable & Radio Corporation
67 Broad Street
New York 4, N. Y.

Congratulations from President Eisenhower to de Forest on the fiftieth anniversary of his invention of the vacuum tube

An early installation of the Poulsen arc system was established between San Francisco and Los Angeles. This was completed and in operation before 1911. Its speed of message transmission was relatively slow, probably because of the characteristics of the Poulsen arc. Some improvements in the keying system were developed by Fuller, Logwood, and Elwell but did not completely solve the problems.

In July 1911, Federal employed Lee de Forest, who had invented the three-element vacuum tube, to devise ways to improve the rate of transmission. About that time the affairs of de Forest were at a low ebb and he was glad to take a position with Federal at a salary of $300 per month. During the period of his employment, which ended May 1, 1913, he made improvements to the San Francisco-to-Los Angeles Poulsen system and greatly increased the message speed.

As a result of the successful San Francisco-to-Los Angeles system, Federal entered into a contract with China to deliver six Poulsen arc units to that country. The dates involved are not clear from the available records, but probably the contract was entered into after 1913 and sometime before 1920. The units were constructed by Federal and crated for shipment to China. At the time of my first visit to the offices and laboratory in Palo Alto (1925) six crates were in a lot next to the main building and it was explained to me that they were Poulsen arc units that had been built for China, but that delivery to China had been prevented by the Boxer rebellion. Except for two of the units, what became of the remaining units is something of a mystery. One of the two units was donated to the University of California, where the magnet was used by Dr. Lawrence to build his first cyclotron. Another one is now on display in the Electronics Museum of Stanford University. Many of the arc transmitters sold by Federal, such as the one installed in Arlington, Virginia, operated successfully.

In the period after I arrived in San Francisco, Federal conducted research and development on several projects. It organized the Kolster Radio Company to develop and market home broadcast radio receivers. On the basis of early radio-compass patents acquired by Kolster before and during his early work with the

National Bureau of Standards in Washington, D.C., a project was carried out to develop commercial radio-compass systems for marine use. A second project was the development of radio transmission and receiving systems suitable for marine service, particularly for Mackay Radio. A third project was an extensive program that followed confirmation of Federal's nonexclusive rights to important patents issued to Lee de Forest and based on inventions made while he was employed by Federal, including the oscillating Audion, which was a three-element vacuum tube in an oscillator circuit—an essential part of any practical radio transmitter. The Poulsen arc system was considered obsolete and of no commercial value, particularly because the vacuum tube was proving to be highly efficient and versatile for radio transmitters as well as receivers.

Federal Telegraph facility on El Camino Real in Palo Alto

As related more fully in the chapter on Frederick A. Kolster, in the early twenties Federal reviewed its position with respect to inventions made by Lee de Forest while an employee of Federal during the period of July, 1911 to May, 1913. Only later did it become known that during his employment he invented the oscillating Audion, the cascade amplifier, and the grid leak. Federal's patent attorney, after reviewing the pertinent documents and files, was of the opinion that, with the exception of possible "shop rights," Federal could not establish ownership of patent rights on these inventions, although at the time of his employment he had contracted to assign all such patent rights to Federal. One of my early work assignments was to review the previous opinion and the pertinent documents and give a new, independent opinion of Federal's rights. As a result of my opinion, in the latter part of 1925 or the early part of 1926 Federal presented its position to American Telephone & Telegraph and General Electric and as a result was granted a nonexclusive royalty-free license to commercialize the inventions made by de Forest during the term of his employment with Federal, including the oscillating Audion.

Upon reviewing the subject matter of the de Forest applications and patents involved, the engineers of Federal decided that they could proceed to develop acceptable commercial radio transmitters and receivers for marine service, and radio broadcast receivers for home use.

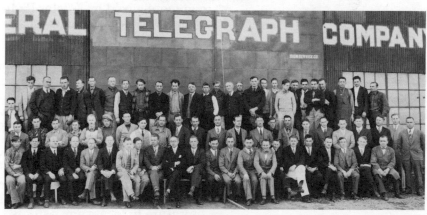

Early employees of Federal Telegraph

Because of the various research and development projects undertaken by Federal, eventually as many as 20 or more engineers were hired and worked on various projects at the Palo Alto laboratory. A complete list of these engineers is not available, but it includes the following:

Ralph R. Beal	Charles V. Litton
William M. Brower	James A. Miller
Archibald S. Brown	H. E. Overacker
Paul F. Byrne	George T. Royden
Gilbert W. Cottell	Ralph Shermund
Harold F. Elliott	Sigurd A. Sollie
Gerhard R. Fisher	Hans Otto Storm
Valentine F. Greaves	Eldridge Z. Stowell
Frederick A. Kolster	Clinton H. Suydam
Geoffrey G. Kruesi	Claude T. Woodard

As the development work proceeded, Kolster very quickly developed acceptable commercial prototypes of radio compasses. His early patents, developed while he was with the U.S. Bureau of Standards, featured the use of a coiled or looped wire as a directional antenna. The improvements made while he was with Federal included an adjustable cam arrangement that compensated for the presence of metallic masses, which had a distorting effect on the compass readings. Another improvement employed complete shielding of the coiled antenna (Patent 1,673,248). Sensitive circuitry was developed that made use of the improved three-element vacuum tube then being produced by General Electric. Commercialization of the Kolster radio compass was relatively extensive, although no records are available to show actual sales.

Kolster was also largely responsible for the development of the Kolster radio broadcast receivers for home use. The receiver was commercialized by Kolster Radio Company, which was organized as an affiliate or subsidiary of Federal. The receiver was characterized by the use of a gang condenser, or in other words a plurality of condensers or capacitors mounted on a common shaft, and a drum-type indicating dial. It also incorporated special circuitry so that the tuning sensitivity remained constant over the entire broadcast frequency range.

The development of commercial radio equipment for marine service proved to be more difficult. As tentative circuitry was proposed, searches were made in the patent literature to locate any patents that might be infringed. This procedure continued for a period of more than one year, during which many searches and many reports were made with respect to patentability and the possibility of infringement.

It was necessary to develop the transmitters and receivers for operation in the short-wave frequency range that had been exploited by the great inventor Fessenden. The de Forest inventions and patents licensed to Federal did not deal with short-wave systems. Investigations revealed many patents in this field which were difficult to avoid in the design of both transmitters and receivers.

Although the general public remembers very little about the history of Federal, they do

Huge parabolic reflector used by Dr. Kolster in 1928 for research with short-wave directional antennas.

remember what was known as "the copper kettle." During Kolster's research work on short-wave transmitters and receivers, he engineered the construction of a large parabolic reflector made of copper. As I remember the dimensions it was about 10 to 12 feet in diameter and was mounted about 15 feet above ground level. A short-wave generator was coupled to a dipole antenna that was mounted within and aligned with the axis of the reflector. The experimental installation was on a vacant lot beside Federal's Palo Alto building, located near the corner of University Avenue and El Camino Real. It created much public interest, and even now if one speaks of the Federal Telegraph Company, there is frequent reference to the copper kettle. The engineers were amazed at the transmitting range obtained with the equipment. Kolster attributed its performance to the reflection of the transmitted beam between the Heavyside layer and the Earth's surface. Clear signals were received as far away as England, using very little power.

Kolster's "Copper Kettle"

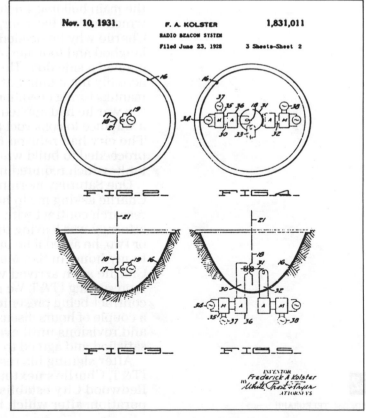

During the period from the Fall of 1926 to 1931, I was actively involved in all the patent application work and patent investigations. My last assignment was to prepare an application for an invention of Charles Litton. When I arrived at the Palo Alto laboratory in late 1929 I was introduced to Litton, and he proceeded to explain the features of the transmitter tube design he had developed that utilized cooling liquid. In the succeeding years Litton became well known among the California electronic companies, and during World War II he had an extensive operation in Redwood City, California, where he developed machinery for constructing and evacuating transmitting and receiving tubes. Particularly he became known for his so-called "glass lathe," which was used in the manufacture of various vacuum tubes.

I had no further contact with Litton until shortly after the war when I had occasion to visit his Redwood City establishment. At that time Charlie had ceased all manufacturing operations, and was endeavoring to decide what his future activity might be. Aside from the main building, I noted a cylindrical building which looked like a large water tank. I asked Charlie why he needed such a large tank. He laughed and took me over to the "tank" and opened a side door. He explained that it was actually not a tank but another building for manufacturing operations. It seems that during the war he had applied to the city fathers for a variance to construct another plant building. The city had refused the variance, so he proceeded to build what he termed a water tank—which required no variance.

One Saturday morning I received a call from Charlie asking me to help him negotiate a research contract with IT&T. Since the IT&T attorney was leaving the city within a day or two, he asked if he might come immediately to my home in San Mateo. I agreed, and Charlie soon arrived with the attorney representing IT&T. We reviewed the research contract being presented by IT&T, spending a couple of hours discussing various changes and revisions until eventually Charlie was satisfied and agreed to sign a retyped copy.

After signing his research contract with IT&T, Charlie's next move was to sell his Redwood City establishment and his corporation, after which he organized a new group to handle research projects originating with IT&T. Instead of remaining in Redwood City, he financed a building in Grass Valley, California, in the foothills of the Sierra Nevada, where he proceeded for several years to carry out substantial research for IT&T.

I have not been able to follow the careers of the other Federal engineers but many of them remained in California after IT&T's acquisition of Federal. Leonard Fuller, who was a company officer and in general charge of Federal's research operations in Palo Alto, became head of the Electrical Engineering Department of the University of California at Berkeley.

By the time Federal was acquired by IT&T, Kolster Radio Company was no longer active. Although its radio receivers had a fair initial acceptance, they met with severe competition that made manufacture uneconomical. Kolster at one time told me that the retail price of the receivers was about four times greater than Kolster Radio's factory price.

I like to believe that Federal left a valuable legacy to California. It initiated serious research in the field of electronics and communications, and although its operations came to an end, such research was soon picked up by others, including former Federal personnel who remained in California.

René Jean-Marie Gaubert

Plastic Bag Making

René Gaubert

RENÉ GAUBERT IS A CLASSIC example of an immigrant who made good in America. I first met René when he was a young man, not long in the United States. During the years of our later association he told me about coming to the United States from his native France.

René was born January 12, 1901, and raised in the French town of Villefranche, in the Department of Aveyron. His father was a lawyer and his mother a doctor. He attended the French public schools, graduating from grammar school in September, 1913 (comparable to the first year of high school in the United States).

On October 5, 1913 he and his parents came to America. After one week in America he attended school, but dropped out after one month. He got a job in a drugstore in Berkeley but since he did not speak English the job lasted only one day. His next job in a jewelry store lasted about six days. Finally at a French laundry he was able to keep a job, running a body ironer ten hours a day, six days a week at $10 per week.

A couple of years later, when America went to war, two of René's older brothers joined the U.S. Army and were being sent to France. One of them suggested to René that since he loved mechanics he should get a job in a machine shop. His first job at such work was at the Union Gas Engine Company as an apprentice. As told by René, after a few months he went to his foreman and said, "I know what I am doing. I want to change jobs." The foreman said, "You are never satisfied. We have changed your job many times. I cannot change it again for a while," so René said, "I quit." He soon found work at Dow Pump in

Alameda, telling them he had four years of experience. Here again the same scenario was repeated. His next job was as a full-fledged machinist, at Bethlehem in Alameda where about two thousand people were building engines for Liberty ships. He worked there for several years, until the war ended. By that time there were only about a half dozen people left at the plant. René recalls that his foreman, Jack Mello, said, "We are hoping to change our business to building engines for domestic purposes. I will keep in touch with you, but must lay you off at this time." After waiting four months René called Jack, who told him to find another job since things did not look good there.

After a few months at Caterpillar Tractor Company in San Leandro he located a job through a friend at Johnson Gear Company in Berkeley, where he was told that the work was interesting as well as difficult. He remembered that a Mr. Brown of Johnson Gear asked him many questions, finally saying, "I believe we can hire you, but want you to know that last week we fired twelve people on this job. Are you still interested?" René said, "I'll take the thirteenth chance." Mr. Brown smiled and said, "Come to work tomorrow at eight."

His foreman, Fred Trevorow, told René later that for two or three weeks he was ready to fire him. He saw that René was spoiling a lot of work because he wanted to go too fast. He thought René would overcome this with time, which he did.

Eventually, when somebody would come in with an idea or invention, René would be assigned to build what they wanted and help them to be successful. This involved analyzing the inventor's ideas and considering how they might be improved. He would often take the drawings home and scrutinize them, then go back to the inventor and say "Did you think of doing it like this?" but letting them think it was their idea—it was René's pleasure.

Following the stock market crash and during the Great Depression René's working time at Johnson Gear was reduced by one day. René decided to take Mondays off. About that time he learned that his uncle, Paul Lavergne, was working to develop a pie wrapper. René took a look at the wrapper and immediately decided that it could be simplified and improved. He quit his job at Johnson Gear with the explanation that he had a new job "working for himself." This was probably one of the most important decisions of his life.

In a few months René designed and built a machine that not only wrapped pies with cellophane but also removed the pie plate automatically before wrapping. A patent application was filed on the machine in December 1932, in the joint names of Lavergne and René (U.S. Patent 2,022,425). This was René's first patent experience.

René built a few of these pie-wrapping machines in a small shop that he had set up in his basement, selling one of them to a local bakery. While discussing the matter of promoting sales of the machines with Zellerbach Paper Company, he was advised to contact their Los Angeles division by someone who thought they might be interested in buying the machine. Zellerbach's southern division liked the machine, but they did not choose to buy it. However, they assigned one of their salesmen to René to enable him to carry out a sales campaign covering Southern California. This campaign was reasonably successful in that he sold a machine every day for over a period of about twenty days, during which time he made sales contacts in such places as Ventura, San Bernardino, and Los Angeles. In general it was a very successful trip. He was then advised by Zellerbach to go East, past the Mississippi, "where all the people are."

René made fifteen pie-wrapping machines, and with his wife took off for their big trip. In Sacramento he sold one machine. They moved on and he stopped in Lafayette, Indiana. It was a beautiful day and René told his wife they were going to have a picnic. After purchasing some salami, French bread, and wine, he passed a pie shop and, thinking it would be nice to have a pie, he entered the shop. Looking at the pies it occurred to him that he might make a sale if he could see the manager, a Mr. Williams. After many attempts to see the manager, René's persistence finally paid off and Mr. Williams came into the shop. Immediately he became very interested in René's machine. Since he was on his way to the Purdue University football game he asked René to leave his machine and, taking his address, said he would either return the machine or send him the money for it. Williams also advised René that when he reached Chicago he should attend the packaging show to exhibit his machine.

While in Chicago René was unsuccessful and failed to sell even one machine. In Albany he found a small pie shop where he showed his machine. The proprietor liked the machine and said he would send René a check. He sent several, all of which bounced. Going back to Albany several months later René saw his machine in the shop window, but the shop had gone bankrupt.

On the way to New York they went to Long Island and stayed with friends who lived in Long Island City. After arriving in New York City René first went to the office of DuPont, where he was given several addresses of prospective customers. DuPont then asked René to call on a man by the name of Kinkanen at Continental Baking Company, whose office was at Rockefeller Center. Kinkanen received him enthusiastically but unfortunately Continental was not wrapping pies. Still he urged René to stop and see him whenever he came to New York again.

After twelve months in New York and the surrounding areas, René had not been able to sell any machines. Finally he told his wife, "We must go home, we've been here one year. Let's make arrangements and leave within one week." René went to say goodbye to Mr. Kinkanen, explaining that he could not afford to stay any longer and thanking him for his help. Kinkanen thought for a while and said, "René, if you could make your little machine wrap the 'Hostess' cakes, we might be interested. I don't see how you can do it, but let's hope you can." René said, "Mr. Kinkanen, I'm going to think about it like hell until I do it."

René purchased a drafting board, squares, pencil, paper, and other supplies for three dollars. In the basement of his friend's house he set up a bench and drafting table. It took two to three weeks to make the changes and practically redesign the whole machine. It was necessary to make the plate on which the cakes were put, one side cold and the other side hot, to make the seal. He arranged for use of a machine shop on Queens Boulevard for ten cents an hour, and two months later he went to see his friend Kinkanen with the new machine. René could wrap the cakes from five inches diameter up to ten inches and the machine was adjustable for height. René relates what happened during the ensuing demonstration:

I placed the little machine on his mahogany desk. He asked me if I could wrap six-inch cakes and I said yes. He called the office downstairs where they were making samples, and he ordered a tray with six-inch Hostess cakes. I had several sheets of cellophane with me, of all sizes. I picked out sheets which were suitable for the six-inch cakes, and I wrapped a cake for him. Kinkanen looked at the beautifully wrapped package, with pleats on the side, and he asked me the size of the cellophane sheet and said, "We will save ten percent off of the size sheet we are now using." He made me wrap the whole tray, and he called the Hoboken, New Jersey, Continental factory and told the supervisor that he must produce 500 six-inch cakes for testing the machine. I was told to have DuPont ship a thousand sheets of cellophane for the test. Then he said I should pick him up at nine o'clock the next morning to go to Hoboken.

The next morning I picked him up and we went to Hoboken, and the supervisor was very intrigued. We got everything ready to go, waited a little for the heater to get hot, and I wrapped a few cakes and I was asked to pick out a girl now wrapping by hand on the line. I did, and I wrapped some cakes very slowly and told her to do it slowly. After I had wrapped about fifty she said, "I think I can do it now." I checked every move she made, and saw that she was gradually speeding up and I boosted the heat. She wound up going almost twice as fast as I had. After about a half an hour, Mr. Kinkanen said, "René, take me to my office." When we got there he said, "You call me tomorrow at nine." When I called, he said, "René, how soon can you ship us six more machines?" I told him it would be about three weeks.

When the packages were seen on the market, I got calls from other bakeries and sold a few, and then decided to go home. I went to see my friend and thanked him for what he had done for me, which I would never forget. He said, "Before you leave, I will mail you a copy of the letter I sent to all the Continental branches between here and San Francisco." Later I sold nine machines to Jack Goldie, manager of the

Continental Baking branch in San Francisco. The market for pie machines went to practically nothing, due to the high cost of cellophane, and the market for cake-wrapping machines also kept going down.

René also tells about his work near the end of his stay in New York City as follows.

One day the maintenance man from Continental called me and said he had a problem with one of my machines and asked me to come over as soon as possible and bring a certain spring. I was working on this machine when the manager, Jack Goldie, came by and said "When you get through, come to my office. I want to talk to you." He opened the door and I went to sit on the couch. He said, "René, do you want to make $50,000?" I smiled but said nothing. He said, "Come here," and he opened a drawer of his desk and pulled out a sheet of heat sealing M.S.T. cellophane and said, "I have been trying to make a small hand machine that would make a heat-sealed bag out of this sheet of cellophane." When I asked him why he wanted to do this when there are very good machines that can produce cellophane glued bags very fast, he said, "You see that sheet there? I can buy these sheets for five dollars per thousand. For the glued bags it costs me twenty-five dollars per thousand. I want to pack my cookies in a cellophane bag but can't afford it. I know you can do it and you'll make fifty thousand dollars. It does not have to be fast as I pay my girls 50 cents per hour."

By the time I got home, I had figured out a rough way to do the job. About a month later I had built a model and prepared a few bags. I wrote to DuPont and told them about this, and that I would appreciate their cooperation. Their reply said, "You're crazy. This won't work. We will not cooperate." I immediately took this letter to Jack Goldie. He said, "The hell with DuPont. How are you getting along?" I said I needed another month. "I am now working on making a machine with a motor drive to automate some functions."

René first built a simple, semi-automatic machine that was capable of manufacturing cellophane bags of varying sizes—bags actually superior to those being bought from eastern sources. He secured a patent on this machine

(Patent 2,094,594), and began its manufacture. The machine met with almost instant success and made it possible for René to establish a small shop with creditable manufacturing facilities. Except for actual shop manufacturing, René was the mainstay of his organization. He was his own salesman and sales were direct to the buyer and user. He also supervised manufacture of the machines.

Gaubert demonstrating his bagging machine

After several years of sales of his semi-automatic machine, a fully automatic bag-making machine appeared on the local market. Although it was more expensive than René's simple machine, he rightly judged it to be serious competition. René's reaction was immediately to design his own fully automatic machine and bring an action in the federal courts for infringement of broad claims of his patent. At the infringement trial three machines were demonstrated, namely René's semi-automatic machine, the defendant's fully automatic machine, and the new automatic machine which at that time was being introduced to the trade by René. Although the court, during the course of the trial, proposed a settlement, the defendant refused to take the license that René offered. After conclusion of the trial the court, to our surprise, held the broader claims of the patent invalid.

Despite the availability of the competing machine, René's fully automatic bag-making machine (Patent 2,347,902) was well received. The trade had confidence in René and accepted his performance guarantees. On the other hand, the competitor's fully automatic machine was being made by parties relatively unknown to the trade. René learned that the competitor had an application pending in the Patent Office, and he appreciated that their machine had some features that he might wish to use. During some casual conversations with the defendant, he discovered that they were willing to sell their patent rights. Accordingly he purchased their patent application and whatever business they had developed. About the same time he learned of another party that had also developed a fully automatic machine, but had not manufactured it commercially. Again René purchased their patent rights so that with his own patents and the patent rights that he had purchased, he had a relatively strong patent position.

As early as 1940 René adopted the trade-name "Simplex" for his machines and for his company (Simplex Wrapping Machine Company). The success of his bag-making machines made it possible to extend his shop facilities and hire more employees. Like many hard-driving inventors René continued to supervise all the more important phases of his business, including financing, manufacturing, and sales. He kept in close contact with his customers and became familiar with their operations and problems.

About this time he perceived the need for machines that would not only make bags automatically, but would also fill the bags with measured amounts of a product, such as hard candy or dried fruit. In a relatively short time he developed machines that combined the functions of automatically manufacturing plastic bags, filling the bags with measured amounts of a product and then heat-sealing the upper open end of the bags. These machines opened up a further market with customers who wanted to fully automate these functions.

Later, after selling his bag-making patents and business to Food Machinery Corporation (FMC), René bought a lot and some adjacent land in San Leandro for the purpose of building a small shop. The party that sold him the lot also built the shop. About that time Frank Viola (plant Supervisor of Golden Grain in San Leandro) had occasion to listen to a magnetic tape machine that René had invented. One day he said, "René, I want you to build a machine for me to package spaghetti." René said, "Frank, I'm not interested. I like my music machine too much to do other things." He took René to lunch and on the way back insisted that they stop at Golden Grain. He showed René an operation where about 20 girls weighed the spaghetti and put it in bags, then another person closed each bag. René agreed to think about the operation, and Viola said, "You can't weigh it—just wrap it." Next day René met Viola again and said to him, "I think I can do this but I must weigh it." Viola said, "I don't want you to weigh it." René said, "I don't want to wrap it without weighing it, too," and he left. Viola called him back and said, "OK, do what you want."

The machine that René then developed was, in his words, "one of the most difficult to design." Golden Grain purchased about twelve of the machines. They also were one of René's first customers to purchase printed cellophane for use in the machines.

The spaghetti-wrapping machine that René invented was sufficiently reliable for use in the average spaghetti factory. His machine (Patent 3,109,502) automated several essential functions, including weighing out predetermined amounts of the spaghetti sticks, wrapping the sticks in a sheet of flexible plastic film, securing the wrapper by a longitudinal seal, folding over the projecting ends of the wrapper, and heat-sealing the overlapped end folds. Patent rights to this machine were licensed to a company in Chicago (Triangle Packaging Machine Company). The machine has been widely sold in the United States and foreign countries. René manufactured the machines in his shop in San Leandro, and sold a number of them to spaghetti manufacturers in California.

Gaubert overseeing performance of his spaghetti-wrapping machine

René's son, Claude, was married in June, 1959. During the year following his marriage he worked at an establishment in the southeast. Since he was not happy in that position, René persuaded him to return to California with the promise that he would start a new company that Claude could manage. René started the new company (Packaging Industries, Inc.) in San Leandro, California. The main business of the company was the manufacture of plastic film stock to be sold in bulk. The company also had printing equipment which could print the film with a labeling or embellishment as desired by the customer. Today the company manufactures a variety of plastic film material, including plain, printed, and laminated. The plant is equipped with several film-making machines of the vertical-cylinder draw type. René has used his expertise in the various plant operations and has invented automatic film-splicing equipment for use with the film-printing equipment.

René has one section of the plant where he continues to develop new products. He became interested in wine packages that consist of a fiberboard carton with an inner plastic bag. Such wine packages were first popularized in Australia. The inner plastic bag has a fitting that can be extended through one carton wall to provide a tap. René built a special machine for such packages (Patent 4,341,522), which he has used to make bags for a number of California wineries. He has built another machine (Patent 4,568,321) for making comparable bags of a much larger size, used for bulk storage of various liquids and concentrates. He has developed a new type of tap assembly that swings down from one wall of the carton to the dispensing position, with simultaneous coupling of the inner end of the tap with the bag.

René's brother, Noel, who immigrated to California with René, was interested in California real estate, and became a building designer and contractor. He interested René in acquiring real estate in Oakland, and in various building projects. One project was an apartment complex built strictly in French style which might pass for a Parisian building. At the time René took me for a tour of the place, we went through the apartment where he lived, and also through the recreation facilities at the top of the building. He explained that the facilities were for the use of any of the tenants, free of charge. Incidentally, he mentioned that he enjoyed 100% occupancy.

René's story again demonstrates that inventions and patents can play an important part in building new industries. Credit must also be given to the general social atmosphere that is present on the Pacific Coast, which is conducive to creation and commercialization of new things. If René had remained in France the possibilities are that he would not have become an inventor.

By actual count, René Gaubert has made more than thirty-five inventions on which patents have been issued in the United States. Only one of the patents has been involved in any litigation.

Charles P. Ginsburg

Video Tape Recorder

THE INVENTION OF THE VIDEO tape recorder, which revolutionized the television industry, is also discussed in the chapter about Alexander Poniatoff and mentioned elsewhere in this book, since several engineers contributed to the final product. It was Charles P. Ginsburg, however, who headed the research and development from the beginning and to the production of a commercial prototype. Throughout the period, beginning with construction of the first tested model in 1952, he served as project engineer for a group consisting, at first, of Ray Dolby and himself, and later expanded to include Charles E. Anderson, Alex Maxey, Shelby Henderson, and Fred Pfost.

Ginsburg received a Bachelor's degree in a combination of mathematics and engineering from San Jose State College (later University) in California. Before and during his attendance at San Jose State he worked in the radio broadcasting industry for more than ten years. He became an employee of Ampex in Redwood City, California in 1951. He became a vice president of Ampex in 1959, and retired at the end of January 1986.

In 1951, Alex Poniatoff, together with Walter T. Selsted, then chief engineer of Ampex, and Myron Stolaroff, gave serious consideration to the development of a video tape recorder. By that time, Radio Corporation of America (RCA) had demonstrated that it was possible to record and reproduce video tape images by the use of a high-speed magnetic tape machine of conventional design. However, that approach was not considered practical for a commercial machine. About that time Stolaroff talked about developing a different type of recorder with Marvin Camras of Armour Reseach Foundation. They discussed the possible use of a rotary head assembly for lateral scanning across a magnetic tape instead of scanning lengthwise. Ampex, at that time, was a licensee

Charles P. Ginsburg

of Armour under numerous Armour patents pertaining to sound recording on magnetic tape. As a result of their discussions, a project was authorized by Ampex in December of 1951 to develop a video tape recorder making use of a rotary scanning head. Ginsburg was selected to pursue the project.

About the same time a search was conducted to locate any U.S. patents pertaining to video tape recorders. The search did not find any U.S. patents on video recorders, but it did find U.S. Patent 2,916,546, which disclosed a crude tape recorder using a rotary head assembly for sound recording. The inventor was an Italian and the invention originated in that country. I advised that in my opinion the patent would not be infringed by a video recorder, since it was anticipated that the rotary head would function only for video signals. Sound would be recorded lengthwise on the tape.

In May of 1952, Ginsburg's preliminary work was interrupted by a crash program to which he was diverted. He believes this was a fortunate interruption because it put him in contact with Ray Dolby, a part-time Ampex employee who became an important asset to the project. At the time of his employment in 1952, Dolby was 17 years of age and had not yet graduated from high school. He had no formal engineering education but he did have a pronounced aptitude for technical matters. He was drafted into the Army in March 1953. However, after his discharge from military service, Dolby again became a part-time employee of Ampex, and was again assigned to the project.

During 1952, it was my custom to make frequent visits to Ampex in Redwood City to discuss with Alex Poniatoff new inventions and developments being made by employees. During one of these visits, in November 1952, Alex said that Ginsburg and Dolby had assembled video recording equipment and that they might be able to make a demonstration. We then went next door and Alex introduced me to Ginsburg and Dolby. Ginsburg explained the equipment which included a number of components arranged on a breadboard. Particularly he described the rotating head assembly, the transport for moving the tape past the heads, and the nature of the electronic circuitry. They produced a

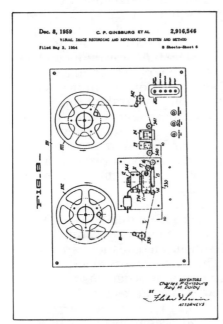

Illustrations from Ginsburg and Dolby's Patent 2,916,546, "Visual Image Recording and Reproducing System and Method"

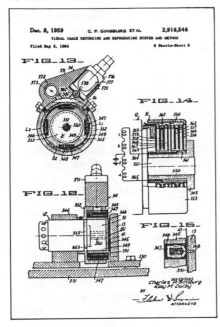

two-inch-wide tape which had previously been recorded from a black-and-white broadcast program. The electronic portion of the recorder was connected to a television screen. The operation produced a recognizable video picture that was far from perfect but clearly demonstrated to both Alex and me that the system was workable.

During the conversation following the demonstration, we asked about improvements that might be made. They impressed us by describing a number of improvements that they had already planned to make, and which they believed would greatly improve the fidelity of the image. A U.S. patent application was filed May 3, 1954 in the names of Ginsburg and Dolby as joint inventors, and was based upon this first equipment plus some improvements. One phase of the application issued as Patent 2,916,546 on December 8, 1959.

After the November 19, 1952 demonstration, it was recognized that much work would have to be done to produce images of high quality and, in general, to provide apparatus that would meet the rather stringent requirements of the television networks.

A second system was completed in March of 1953. Some improvements were incorporated, including a new rotary head assembly consisting of four magnetic heads mounted on the plane face of the rotary drum. As with the first equipment, the heads were arranged to sweep across a two-inch-wide tape along arcuate paths. An amplitude modulation system was used. The rotary head assembly included a photocell, which received reflected light pulses from a light source focused on a rotating guide ring. This produced a 300-cycle photocell drive signal which was recorded on one edge of the tape by means of a conventional stationary head. During playback, the 300-cycle signal from the tape was used as the input signal to drive and control the amplifier that drove the drum motor.

Although the second system was better in performance than the earlier system, Ginsburg recognized that additional problems required solving before the system could be commercialized. Ginsburg and Anderson made some changes in the control system, and demonstrated the equipment in September 1954 to a management committee. The committee was favorably impressed and further development was authorized.

During the next development phase, some changes were made that proved to be of major importance. The tape was cupped to conform with the periphery of the rotating drum. The magnetic heads on the drum swept laterally across the tape in straight lines. Ginsburg refered to these changes as "new geometry." Pictures made with the new geometry in December 1954 showed marked improvement, particularly with respect to stability. However, it was apparent that some problems still existed.

During all the above development, the recorder used amplitude modulation (AM). In December 1954 the use of a vestigial sideband FM (frequency modulation) system was proposed. The circuitry was modified to use the FM system, and was demonstrated in February 1955 with good results.

U.S. Patent 2,956,114 covers the carrier frequency modulated system now being used by all commercial video tape recorders. The patent names Ginsburg, Henderson, Dolby, and Anderson as joint inventors. The patent was referred to by the United States Patent Office in their booklet entitled "Revolutionary Ideas—Patents and Progress in America" in their list of "important patents."

On March 2, 1955 a very convincing demonstration was made for the Ampex Board of Directors. During the month that followed careful deliberation raised many questions, all of which had to be answered with reasonable accuracy to successfully proceed from breadboard demonstrations to a commercially acceptable product. The group then proceeded under a new authorization that stated the objective of having a system for public demonstration within one year.

In after-hours experiments during February of 1955, Alex Maxey discovered some very significant phenomena connected with the characteristics of pictures reproduced from tape. He found that the amount of information read out during playback by each of the heads per unit of arc sweep could be controlled by varying the tape tension in any one of three ways: at the reels, by moving the female guide toward or away from the rotating drum, or by varying a partial vacuum that was developed by sucking air from the noncontact side of the tape.

Although the group was concerned with the extent of the nonlinearities that might be introduced by using the guide position as an information rate control, it was determined experimentally that the nonlinearity caused by the vacuum method was not objectionable. This technique of varying the tape tension proved to be one of the major breakthroughs in the program. It provided an excellent solution for the problem of information rate changing as the heads wore down to a smaller sweep radius, and it gave an answer to a part of the question of ultimate interchange-ability of recorded tapes from one machine to another.

An entirely new head development program was carried on by Fred Pfost. He made radical changes in the design of the individual magnetic heads, using a sandwich-type construction that provided the necessary mechanical support and was highly repro-ducible as well. The work on heads during this period was done in a much more analytical fashion than before.

The modulation system was extended in bandwidth so that it would be suitable to operate with a carrier frequency of as high as six megacycles, if such an operating frequency should turn out to be usable. The switching unit, which had previously been a two-mode device, was replaced by a four-way switcher that would allow only one channel at a time to conduct. Considerable improvements were made in resolution and in signal-to-noise ratio. The drum was stabilized sufficiently to allow the display of pictures from tape on a standard monitor. No attempt was made during this period to redesign the recorder for commercial use. The breadboard consisted of a crude wooden cabinet containing the top plate and electronic chassis, operating in conjunction with two partially full racks. At a demonstration given for some officers of the firm toward the end of 1955, it was suggested that a more attractive package should be developed for what would be a very expensive recorder. Accordingly, Anderson began the design of the Mark IV console with its compact rack arrangement. It was also decided that plans should be directed toward a surprise demonstration at the National Association of Radio and Television Broadcasters (NARTB) convention in Chicago in April of 1956.

In early February of 1956, a demonstration was given for what was originally presumed to be a very small management group but turned out to be attended by about 30 Ampex people. For all personnel on the engineering project, this was a most dramatic demonstration. The guests arrived, were seated, a few words were spoken to the effect that they would see the results of the work to date, and the recorder was then put in the playback mode and showed a program recorded an hour earlier. It was then announced that a sequence would be recorded and immediately played back. A program was recorded for about two minutes. The tape was rewound and stopped, and then the playback button pushed. Although completely silent up to this point, the entire group rose to its feet and shook the building with applause and shouting.

Original six members of the video tape recorder development team with the Mark IV prototype in 1956. From left to right: Fred Pfost, Shelby Henderson, Ray Dolby, Alex Maxey, Charles Ginsburg, and Charles Anderson

Ampex had many visitors during the next few weeks, including Bill Lodge of CBS, Frank Marx of ABC, and representatives of CBC and BBC. The visitors were all sworn to secrecy and ushered in and out separately so that they would not see each other. As a result of

Lodge's visit, arrangements were made to use the Mark IV model, which had not yet been assembled, for a surprise showing to the annual CBS affiliates meeting that was to occur the day before the formal opening of the NARTB convention in Chicago.

With only about six weeks left before the convention, working hours were extended to complete the construction of Mark IV and at the same time to continue development work so that the picture to be demonstrated in Chicago would be as good as CBS was expecting it to be. The pace of activity became furious. The administrative engineer for the group, which by then numbered about a dozen people, spent most of his regular time plus nights and weekends modifying mounting brackets for the Mark IV console, making cable assemblies, and building up redesigned electronic components.

A three-year-old idea of placing the switching transients in the horizontal blanking interval was rushed into hardware form as the blanking switcher, and integrated into the basic system as a toggle-switch option. An automatic rotary head degaussing system was devised to eliminate the need to manually demagnetize the video heads after a recording operation and prior to playback.

Meanwhile it had been decided that Mark III, the machine used for the demonstration in February, should be used for a press demonstration in Redwood City, California, on the same day that the NARTB showing was to start. Therefore, while Mark IV was being used for development work, Mark III had to be prepared for its press appearance.

At last Mark IV was completed, debugged, and then broken down into many pieces and shipped to Chicago. Three days before the press demonstration, Mark III was in severe trouble. Those of the group who were headed for Chicago took off, wishing the stay-at-homes good luck and trying not to think about their difficulties.

The demonstrations were scheduled for Saturday. By Thursday afternoon, Mark IV was assembled in Chicago and making the best pictures ever seen from tape. A predictable situation then occurred. The CBS engineering staff said the pictures were not good enough. The signal-to-noise ratio was too low and the noise banding was unacceptable.

Between Thursday night and Friday night, the crew accomplished what some engineers might well have considered impossible. By cutting, trimming and adjusting, and aided by the last-minute delivery of some tape samples that greatly exceeded in performance anything they had seen before, everyone was satisfied. Checking with the crew in Redwood City, it was found that they had solved their mechanical problems and were now ready for the simultaneous Mark III demonstration.

The demonstrations were a bombshell in the industry. In Redwood City the performance was sensational. In Chicago, pandemonium broke loose and Ampex was flooded with orders. From the time of the CBS affiliates meeting on Saturday morning, and throughout the demonstrations that extended until the following Thursday afternoon for the convention delegates in general, the recorder performed better than anyone had any right to expect.

Four months before the Redwood City and Chicago demonstrations, Ampex had expected to deliver five prototype VTRs to customers in government agencies for evaluation, along with a program leading to gradual delivery of machines for television use starting in 1957. The group now found itself faced with the pressure of making sixteen hand-built machines, most of them going to broadcasters for immediate on-the-air use. At the same time Ampex had to gear up for full-scale commercial production of units that the industry was eager to put to work.

In spite of the good pictures demonstrated in April of 1956, many tasks had to be carried out before releasing the first machine for commercial use. Until then, neither manpower, machine facilities nor technical advances were sufficient to properly evaluate magnetic tape for video tape recording use. Until means could be devised to rate the tape manufacturers' samples with quantitative evaluations rather than with such subjective appraisals as "too many dropouts," or "doesn't wear well," not too much could be accomplished toward getting really satisfactory tape.

The tape-evaluation program consumed many hundreds of manhours and was the cause of severe headaches to the tape manufacturers, to Ampex, and to early network customers. With a then-predicted head life of

Ampex was awarded an Emmy in 1957 for the creation of a practical method of recording television programs on magnetic tape

100 hours, Ampex could not continue to make magnetic heads in a tedious one-at-a-time fashion. The many parameters in head construction, several of which had been varied in cut and try fashion to squeeze out a few more decibels of signal for the April demonstrations, had to be fixed in order to establish Ampex standards before the delivery of the first machines. At the same time, head construction had to be transformed into a semi-production process rather than a handcrafting technique.

In general, the picture reproduced from tape had to be greatly improved over that shown in April with respect to noise, resolution, overshoot and ringing, and horizontal stability. The entire machine had to be repackaged and tested. The mechanical design details were endless. The top plate components had to be not only reliable but also completely interchangeable. And always there was the continuing struggle for greater bandwidth and better signal-to-noise ratio. The length of work days peaked in October and November, and many times during this period a crew of two or three engineers would start a "day" at eight in the morning and finish 30 hours later!

The video tape recorder went on the air for the first time on November 30, 1958, from CBS Television City in Los Angeles. NBC followed suit at the very beginning of 1959, and ABC started delayed telecasts from tape at the beginning of daylight saving time in April of 1959.

One might assume that when manufacture and delivery of the successful recorder was under way there was little more to be done except for designing special adaptations and taking care of customers' problems. However, all the research and development up to that time was to record in black and white. The thinking was that although RCA was spending millions to develop and introduce color television, black and white would remain the prevailing system for a long time. RCA's promotion on color television did not simply require the development of color television transmitters and receivers. It also required drastic changes in broadcast television stations, station programming, studio practices—in general, the revision of the entire broadcasting system of the United States. Any engineer knowing the problems involved might well have concluded that color television was a long way off.

Early in 1957 an officer of Ampex was contacted by an RCA official and was informed that RCA had perfected a color television recorder that they wished to demonstrate to Ampex. After some consideration of this disturbing news, Ampex agreed upon a date for the demonstration which was to take place at the Camden, New Jersey establishment of RCA, near Philadelphia. During the several months preceding the demonstration, work was carried out under Ginsburg's supervision to demonstrate that the Ampex recorder, with some changes and additions, could function in color.

I accompanied a group of Ampex engineers, including Charles Ginsburg, Walter Selsted, Harold Lindsey, and Myron Stolaroff, on a visit to the RCA laboratory in Camden on August 15, 1957. We were ushered into a room where the demonstration was to take place. The mechanical parts of their recorder, including the rotary head assembly, were mounted near the top of one of the support columns of the room. Enough of the mechanism could be seen to determine that they used much of the essential mechanism of the Ampex recorder. The demonstration was excellent. The colors were vivid and there was no distortion of the images.

After the RCA demonstration, it was thought advisable to consider any proposition RCA might offer in the way of an amicable agreement. At that time it was known that RCA had many U.S. patents and patent applications covering various features of color television. Any color television recorder Ampex might have commercialized based on their black-and-white machine might well have infringed one or more of the RCA patents, particularly considering that the recorder would become part of the RCA color system. After giving careful consideration to the situation, Ampex officials decided to ask RCA for a proposal. It was evident by that time that RCA was suggesting cross-licensing between Ampex and RCA with respect to all pertinent patents and patent applications. Alex Poniatoff and I made arrangements to meet in New York City and at that time I visited the Patent Department of RCA to obtain the draft agreement they were to prepare. After some negotiations, the agreement was executed by both parties. A more detailed account of these events will be found in the chapter on Poniatoff.

Following the agreement with RCA, Ampex gave serious consideration to color television and initiated a research project to develop color equipment for use with the black-and-white recorder as well as a recorder that would function in either black and white or in color. During the preliminary phase of this work one of the partners of our firm, Aldo Test, and I visited the section of the Ampex experimental laboratory involved. Ginsburg proceeded with a mathematical discourse with respect to the degree of precision required for a color television recorder, as compared to the requirements for black and white. Two wall blackboards, each about nine feet long, extended from one corner of the room. For about thirty minutes, during which he filled both boards with mathematical equations, he explained why such precision was necessary. Aldo Test followed his mathematics as it was developed, but it was Greek to me!

The color television group was successful in developing a commercial unit that could be operated either in black or white or in color. Their progress was undoubtedly aided by information they acquired from RCA, and the fact that they could freely adopt features developed by RCA without danger of patent infringement.

Ginsburg is named as inventor or co-inventor in about seventeen U.S. patents and pending patent applications, all assigned to the Ampex Corporation. Since his retirement from Ampex at the end of January 1986, he has been engaged in consulting work. Although most of his work with Ampex has been in the field of magnetic tape recorders, and particularly television recorders, he has also been engaged in research projects on other magnetic tape equipment.

Because of what Ginsburg and his research group accomplished, he received many awards, including: the David Sarnoff Gold Medal of the SMPTE in 1957; the Vladimir K. Zworykin Television Prize of the IRE (now the IEEE) in 1958; the Valdemar Poulsen Gold Medal of the Danish Institute of Technical Sciences in 1960; the Howard N. Potts Medal of the Franklin Institute in 1969; and the John Scott Medal of the Board of Directors of the

Alex M. Poniatoff (left) with Ginsburg

City of Philadelphia in 1970. In addition, he was elected a Fellow of the IEEE; a Fellow, then an Honorary Member, of the SMPTE; an Honorary Fellow of the Royal Television Society; a Life Fellow Member of the Franklin Institute; and a Member of the National Academy of Engineering.

Four members of the original VTR development team twenty years later. From left to right: Ray Dolby, Alex Maxey, Shelby Henderson, and Charles Ginsburg

The story of the video tape recorder demonstrates that a relatively small corporation, such as Ampex, can foster an important new product that is eagerly accepted by the trade and very quickly revolutionizes an important industry. It also demonstrates that one inventor, such as Ginsburg, later joined with other engineers, can successfully tackle a development having highly specialized requirements, many of which become evident only as the development proceeds. Ginsburg and the others making up the group never lost faith in the ultimate success of the project.

Marvin H. Grove

High-Pressure Regulator

THIS CHAPTER IS AN ACCOUNT of an independent inventor who made an invention of great value and then proceeded to develop a substantial, profitable company for its commercialization.

Marvin H. Grove graduated from the Naval Academy at Annapolis in 1919. As a naval officer, starting with ensign and ending as submarine commander, he had various experiences with respect to the power and propulsion equipment for naval vessels, and facilities for storing and supplying compressed air under required pressures. Particularly, his duties during that time (1920-1926) included service on the *U.S.S. Fox* in the Black Sea area, and on the battleship *Florida*. In 1925-26 he attended the Navy Submarine School in New Haven, Connecticut, which qualified him for a submarine command, after which he joined the crew of submarine S-43 at Electric Boat Company, Groton, Connecticut. In 1926 he was stationed in Panama for submarine duty. In 1927 he was ordered to Mare Island in California, to serve as a technical consultant in the building of a new and more modern submarine.

His work at Mare Island gave him intimate knowledge of all kinds of metal working, including bending, welding, torch cutting, and machining. This knowledge was of inestimable value in his later work.

While at Mare Island he also learned about the pneumatic systems and equipment on submarines for supplying air under various pressures for a wide variety of purposes, including the charging of torpedoes, the blowdown of ballast tanks, and the starting of diesel engines, used at that time on all submarines. The compressed air for such purposes was stored in huge bottles at pressures ranging from 2000 to 3500 psi. Pressure-reducing regulators were used to reduce the air pressure to usable values ranging from 10

Marvin H. Grove

to 50 psi. Many of the uses of air at reduced pressure were critical, since pressure that was too high might cause tremendous damage. One example was the blowdown of safety tanks for emergency surfacing of a submarine. If such tanks should be disrupted by excessive air pressure, it would endanger the ship and her personnel.

The pressure-reducing regulators used on submarines as of 1917 were generally known to be unreliable. They functioned to reduce the high-pressure air in two stages in series. The difficulties ranged among substantial variations in delivered pressure, frequent need for maintenance and repairs, excessive size and weight, and general lack of reliability.

At that time it was necessary for all U.S. Navy officers to be examined annually to determine their fitness for continued service. As a result of his annual physical examination in the early Fall of 1931, Grove was ordered to report to the Navy Retirement Board because of certain things discovered in his examination. He had developed an arthritic condition of the neck, which made it painful to move his head. The Examining Board decided that this would interfere with his work on a submarine, because he might not be capable of effectively looking through periscopes when the vessel was pitching and rolling. He was recommended for retirement and relieved of command of an S-44 submarine, effective December 31, 1931.

About the time of his retirement from active duty he became familiar with a regulator invented by another Navy officer. Since it was difficult for him to find employment, he agreed to try to promote the regulator with the general understanding that it was better than what was being used by the Navy. With the prototype regulator furnished by the inventor, he contacted Nordstrom Valve Company, which at that time had a substantial plant in Oakland, making lubricated plug valves. They were interested in pursuing the matter, and an exclusive license was entered into specifying royalties to be paid if the regulator was commercially manufactured and sold. Shortly after the license was executed the Nordstrom Valve Company was acquired by Pittsburgh Equitable Meter Company, in Pittsburgh, Pennsylvania. They were manufacturers of so-called "service" gas regulators that were suitable only for relatively low pressures.

Pittsburgh Equitable Meter Company cancelled the license agreement after their engineers had reviewed the regulator, and had probably tested it and found its defects. This experience was disappointing, but it resulted in Grove's becoming interested in developing a new regulator that would perform satisfactorily and reliably.

Another company in Berkeley, California, Shand and Jurs, had sufficient interest in Grove's work to permit him to use a small room of their shop, and to supply the tools he needed. Together with Tom Gannon, a skilled mechanic, he conducted a series of tests to determine why the prototype failed to work properly, and how to construct a regulator without the bad features of the prototype. At that time he was working with a one-stage regulator, having a dome containing air under pressure in place of a spring for loading the operating diaphragm. A so-called diaphragm plate, which was perforated, extended over the diaphragm to limit its flexing in one direction. All the various constructions tried out, with one exception, did not seem to cure erratic operation. The exception was an arrangement in which the dome was provided with a tightly fitting wooden plug extending entirely across its open end.

After trying to analyze why the wooden plug experiment gave promising results, Grove modified the diaphragm plate by closing the perforations with solder, leaving only one very small hole. This regulator was then taken to Mare Island where he had the privilege of using one of the Navy's shops and its tools for testing.

With the help of a retired mechanic, Grove connected the high-pressure side of the regulator through a hand-operated valve, with high-pressure bottles supplying air at a pressure of about 3500 psi. The low-pressure side was connected to an open-ended pipe about eight feet long, provided with a hand valve at the regulator end. A pressure gauge was connected between the hand valve and the regulator. The dome pressure was then set at a relatively low pressure, namely in the range of about 100 to 400 psi. After closing the low-pressure hand valve, the valve on the high-pressure side was opened, and the pressure gauge on the low-pressure side immediately registered the proper low pressure. To determine how the regulator would respond to changes in the flow of gas from the low-pressure side, the hand valve was adjusted from closed to wide open position. To his amazement the needle of the pressure gauge remained stationary. Grove said that his first reaction was that the pressure gauge was defective. After convincing himself that this was not the case, it became evident that the regulation was so sensitive and accurate that the gauge indicated no pressure change. At the conclusion of the test the regulator was disassembled and the diaphragm plate examined with a magnifying glass. It was apparent that the only communication between the space immediately between the diaphragm and the diaphragm plate, and the dome space, was through the very small hole.

Following the successful testing at Mare Island, Grove decided he would construct another regulator using materials acceptable to the Navy—which would make it possible for him to secure Navy acceptance. First it was necessary to determine the optimum size of the small hole in the diaphragm plate. As a result of experiments it was determined that a 1/64-inch hole would be satisfactory for the size of regulator that he had in mind.

The next step in the development was to find a machine shop that would produce an acceptable prototype for presentation to the Navy to obtain acceptance. The first shop was one that made pressure-reducing valves and components of acetylene welding equipment. After making some parts that were unsatisfactory, they gave up the project. The next shop that he contacted was known as Bin's Machine and Tool Works. They took an interest in making the regulator according to his specifications. They produced three regulators using Navy bronze for the dome and body parts. Upon checking the parts, Grove found that there was a serious misalignment of the valve members. It was necessary for him to scrape certain of the metal surfaces by hand to obtain perfect alignment. One of these regulators was delivered to the Navy and was placed on a submarine to prove it out in service.

Aside from the Navy requirements, Grove knew that there was a need for reliable regulators for use in connection with gas transmission lines. He made calls on Pacific Gas and Electric and Standard Oil Company in an effort to sell his regulator for their purposes. It happened that a subsidiary of Standard Oil Company (now Chevron) had made a gas discovery in a remote part of the San Joaquin Valley, which they wished to connect to their main transmission lines. They needed a reliable regulator to reduce the high-pressure gas from the wellhead to the transmission lines. They needed a regulator that was dependable, and would not be subject to freezing on cold nights. They arranged competitive tests between the Grove regulator and a regulator developed by a firm in Los Angeles. In the arrangement proposed by Grove two regulators were used, one being set at a slightly different pressure from the other. The purpose of this was that if one regulator should freeze and cease to work, the other regulator would take over, affording sufficient time for the first regulator to thaw out. The success of this test immediately became known to other gas companies throughout the United States and almost immediately Grove received inquiries from many other companies with similar problems.

News about the regulator spread rapidly in the oil and gas fields, and unsolicited orders began arriving by phone. Almost overnight Grove found that he had the beginning of a profitable business. For a time Bin's continued to make the regulators, but very soon Grove realized he should establish his own manufacturing organization. By that time Grove had accumulated a considerable amount of capital from the initial sales to the oil and gas companies. Also by that time the Navy had approved the regulator for use on submarines and other naval vessels. He purchased the principal tools and the machinery required, rented space in a small building in Oakland, and hired a few employees. One employee, Harold Wolpman, was a skilled machinist previously with Bin's, who had done work on the first regulators. At that time Grove was operating as a partnership with his wife, under the trade name of Grove Regulator Company. Later the partnership was incorporated under the same name.

One of the first engineers Grove hired was Austin Bryant, who had graduated from the University of California at Berkeley. He was recommended by one of his professors as being an excellent student who had failed to find a position due to the Depression. In an effort to make his own way, Austin had acquired a small chicken farm near Salinas, California. By the time he was offered a position by Grove he was disillusioned over the chicken business and was ready to chuck it all. Grove tells the story about their first meeting on the chicken ranch. Austin had collected a huge pile of chicken manure with the understanding that it would command a good price. Unfortunately, and to his disgust, he could not find a buyer at any price. The hiring of Austin was a fortunate move. He was well versed in design and test methods and became chief engineer of the company's engineering department.

Within a few months after starting his first plant, Grove found it necessary to enlarge his manufacturing operations, and acquired a plant considerably larger and better equipped with machine tools.

For some time before World War II the government was engaged in the so-called Defense Program. The Navy continually increased its purchases of the Grove regulator and there were continual increases in nonmilitary sales as well. Grove saw the possibility of adding new products to his line of regulators. Several new products were developed and successfully sold, including a product known as Flex-flo and a high-pressure steam regulator using some of the principles of the original Grove high-pressure regulator. The Flex-flo product used a rubber sleeve that could be expanded or collapsed about a barrier core. It was capable of functioning as a flow-control valve, pressure-reducing or back-pressure regulator, or a relief valve. The Navy found uses for it on their surface vessels. The high-pressure steam regulator was used on destroyers to reduce steam to lower pressures suitable for auxiliary equipment. Another device was a life-raft release, which was used in the lashing of life rafts carried by ships, releasing the rafts if the ship should sink.

The rapid growth of the business during the defense period again made it necessary to provide more adequate facilities. This led to the construction of the first one of the buildings on Hollis Street in Emeryville, California, now being occupied by the company known as Grove Valve and Regulator.

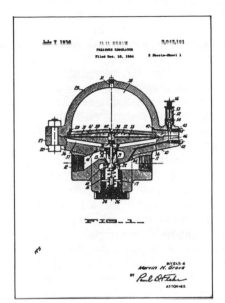

Drawing from Grove's Patent 2,047,101

During the early days of his business Grove had very little involvement in litigation. However, after his business was an obvious success, the two Navy officers for whom he had attempted to sell their unsuccessful regulator demanded that they be made equal partners. Their attorney proposed that this matter be subjected to arbitration. Grove's response was that he would not agree to arbitrate ownership of the business, but he would arbitrate whether or not he should pay a reasonable royalty in the event the arbitrators found that their unsuccessful regulator had contributed to Grove's invention. They elected to go to court, which resulted in litigation lasting over a period of several years. However, the decisions of both the trial and appellate courts were in Grove's favor.

Grove's patent application covering his high-pressure regulator was filed in the Patent Office on December 10, 1934 and was granted as Patent No. 2,047,101 on July 7, 1936. The Patent Office Examiner first held that the regulator was unpatentable but subsequently conceded patentability. With the exception of one instance, the patent was not infringed. The exception involved Grove's first salesman. When Grove terminated his services, the salesman attempted to commercialize a very similar regulator that differed from Grove's only in that instead of a small hole in the diaphragm plate, he employed a leak in the seal between the periphery of the plate and the dome. Before trial the salesman conceded infringement and agreed to a consent decree and injunction.

Sometime after the litigation over ownership of the business, Grove received a copy of a Navy court-martial decision on the question as to whether or not his high-pressure regulator invention was the property of the government, since Grove had been on the inactive list when he made the invention. The decision not only held that Grove had ownership but, in addition, praised the invention as being of great value to the Navy and stated that the Grove regulator was being recommended to all Navy procurement offices. Grove was never advised of pendency of the court-martial proceedings, or the reason why it was instigated.

The World War II period was a very busy one for Grove and the company. By that time

Grove maintained a representative employee in Washington, and made frequent trips to consult with the government purchasing offices. The manufacturing facilities were continually enlarged and improved. A license was granted to a British company, Bell Punch, for the manufacture of the Grove regulator for use by the British military.

During the war Grove was advised that the British were developing improved flame-throwers using napalm fuel. The United States Chemical Warfare Service became involved in the project, and contacted Grove in connection with their regulator requirements. The flamethrower required high-pressure air carried in a bottle or cylinder, and a pressure regulator valve to supply reduced gas pressure to the container that held the napalm fuel. Without Grove's knowledge, they became aware of the Grove pressure regulator valve. In their initial tests it had proven superior to other available pressure regulators. At the request of the Chemical Warfare Service, Grove developed a line of regulators for the different types of flamethrowers. The one for the portable backpack type was made of aluminum and was later sold for commercial purposes under the trade name of "Mighty Mite."

Shell Oil took part in the flamethrower project, and carried out some testing of the larger flamethrowers. They invited Grove and me to their Richmond, California tank farm for a demonstration. The equipment was set up on a hillside about 200 yards from the nearest storage tank. A fair breeze was blowing down the hill toward the tanks. They first shot a salvo of burning napalm in a direction cross-wind and traversing the hill. It worked perfectly, with the burning napalm falling in an area about 150 yards away. They then shot up the hill and against the wind. For a moment the burning fragments appeared to be suspended above us, but eventually they fell a reasonably safe distance away. Their next shot was downhill toward the tank farm. This proved to be poor judgment. The wind carried the fragments much farther than they had anticipated, and they fell in an area very close to one of the tanks. Fortunately a fire-fighting squad was able to quickly extinguish the fragments of burning napalm.

The end of the war came as a shock to the Grove organization. Most government orders were cancelled, although some new orders were received for spare parts. Grove had faith in his ability to develop commercial markets for his products, and to develop new products. Under his direction the Engineering Department, which comprised some 15 to 20 engineers, set about developing various new products that might be commercialized. Grove also launched a completely different project, namely a real estate development. He acquired an undeveloped acreage that was subdivided, and then began building small houses that were sold at prices which today appear to be quite cheap ($12,000-$15,000). As the business of the company improved, Grove lost interest in his real estate development, and eventually sold it.

Grove's Flex-flo device proved to be a product that could be sold for nonmilitary purposes. During the war Grove had concentrated on selling this product to the Navy. Use of Flex-flo and its various applications required a pilot valve, which was a small valve intended to be operated manually or by an electric solenoid. Austin Bryant developed a small valve for this purpose, making use of "O" rings. "O" rings, as of that time, were made of resilient synthetic rubber and were employed to establish a seal between two interfitted parts. The one part had a circular groove that accommodated the "O" ring. Austin not only used such an "O" ring in his small pilot valve, but in addition he added a special feature that enabled the valve to work at relatively high pressures without dislodging the "O" ring.

After recognizing the features of the "O"-ring pilot valve, and particularly its ability to handle high pressures without leakage, Grove undertook with Austin Bryant the development of a gate valve sealed by the use of "O" rings. The common gate valve, as of that time, used a wedge-shaped gate that, when closed, had its sides engaging inclined metal seats. The metal-to-metal seating surfaces did not provide an absolute seal. No matter how tightly the gate was forced between the seats, there was always a slight leakage. After a number of constructions were made and tested, a construction was settled upon that was sealed on both sides of the gate by the use of "O" rings, and which could be used under high pressures and opened and closed without dislodgment of the "O" rings. For what is believed to be the first time, a high-pressure gate valve was made that provided a bubble-tight seal under relatively high pressures. By bubble-tight seal is meant one that is so effective that if the downstream side of the valve is sealed off except for a small tube, and high-pressure air is applied to the upstream side after closing the gate, a water film applied over the end of the tube will not enlarge into a bubble.

Grove undertook to commercialize his new gate valve in the petroleum industry in sizes ranging over several small pipe diameters. The gate of these valves was made flat, and the body was a steel casting. Instead of a conventional packing gland to form a seal about the operating stem of the valve, an "O" ring was again used to establish the seal. These gate valves were well received by the petroleum industry, and used in refineries, on so-called "Christmas tree" assemblies and for other miscellaneous applications.

With his entry into the gate-valve business, particularly in the petroleum industry, Grove appreciated that such business centered in the Texas area. Considering his initial success in marketing his "O"-ring-sealed gate valves, Grove decided to manufacture such valves in larger sizes, such as were used in oil and gas pipeline systems. The valves used in such pipelines range from 12- to 48-inch diameter. Before making this move, cost analyses were prepared to determine the investment required to enter the pipeline-valve field, using valves with cast steel bodies. The costs appeared to be far in excess of his financial assets. However, instead of abandoning the project, Grove set about to develop the manufacture of large gate valves by fabricating methods. Instead of using steel castings, the valve body was made of structural steel, such as steel plates, angles, channels, and so forth, welded together. A number of experimental body constructions were fabricated and pressure-tested. At first the emphasis was on rigidity, which was assumed to mean greater strength. Subsequently, however, it was determined that some flexibility was desirable and that, if properly designed, a structure with flexibility would have the strength to meet the high pressure requirements without having excessive weight.

The first group of pipeline valves was shipped about 1953 or 1954. By that time Grove had undertaken to provide an additional building and equipment for their manufacture, including cranes for handling heavy steel plates, valve bodies, and completed valves, automatic welding equipment of the submerged-arc type, torch cutting equipment, welding jigs and testing equipment. During early development, he found that the flexible body assemblies could be pressurized hydraulically to the point of permanent deformation of certain parts, such as the plates forming the wide sides of the body. It was found that this minimized deflections of the body under normal pipeline pressures. It also simplified machining operations and strengthened the bodies.

Other companies, which at that time were in the pipeline-valve business, were making valves with cast steel bodies and using seals other than the "O"-ring type. The Grove valve with its fabricated body and bubble-tight seal created great interest among competitors and the petroleum industry in the United States and foreign countries. Within a short time Grove's expectations were justified and the company was firmly entrenched in the pipeline-valve business. Essentially the same valve is now being made by Grove Valve and Regulator Company, and is known as the Grove G4 valve.

At various times Grove had occasion to negotiate short-term bank loans. When the banks learned that the business was family-owned, they insisted on his personal guarantee. As the business grew, so did the loans and Grove's personal liability. He became concerned with this situation and finally decided to dispose of the company. By that time he had a separate corporation, Fluid Control, which had been organized for government business. Negotiations with the Walworth Company resulted in purchase of both companies in October 1959 for cash and exchange of Walworth stock. Patent rights to the "O"-ring type of valves were assigned to Walworth, subject to payment of a royalty to Grove. The amount of Walworth stock received was such that the Grove family received about ten percent of the total issued Walworth common stock. After their acquisition, Walworth permitted Grove and his organization to continue to run the company. Grove was elected to the Board of Walworth, which met monthly at Walworth's office in New York City. I joined the Walworth Board a little later.

Not long after Walworth acquired the Grove Valve and Regulator Company, Grove was authorized to grant licenses in England and Italy for the manufacture of the Grove pipe-line valves. After some preliminary corre-spondence with prospective licensees, namely Robert Cort of England and Nuovo Pignone in Italy, it was decided that Grove and I would call on both parties to conclude the arrange-ments. Our wives went along for the trip. We first visited Robert Cort in Reading, England. His firm was familiar with steel fabricating and was looking for new products. The com-pany president, Elder Scouller, a pleasant and capable administrator, had received a draft copy of a proposed license agreement. After visiting the plant, which was an old structure along the Thames River, we went to his office and reviewed the agreement. Within a short time we agreed to certain changes and Scouller's secretary prepared a final revised draft which was executed. Scouller then invited all of us to his newly acquired home for dinner.

We were staying at the Whitehart Inn, a few miles from Reading. We were told that the inn was about two hundred years old, as was indicated by the construction of the doorways, which were about 5½ feet high, just high enough to conk you if you went through without ducking! They had some quaint old customs, such as serving tea in the morning before you were out of bed. Behind the dining room of the inn was a well-kept rose garden that occupied about an acre.

Scouller picked us up at the inn in his old Bentley and took us to his recently acquired home. It was a large house with walls of fieldstone and mortar on a tract that probably amounted to several acres. Scouller's wife was a Greek national, and she was training two young Greek girls as servants. The Scoullers were in the process of furnishing the place, mainly with antiques, but they had not yet found a sideboard for the dining room. After being seated for dinner at a long antique dining table, one of the two Greek girls entered the room with a large tray loaded with china and food. Suddenly she stopped, obviously wondering what to do with the tray. She solved the problem of the missing sideboard by putting the tray on the floor, where it stayed until the items were transferred to the table.

After our negotiations with Robert Cort were completed, we proceeded to Milan, Italy where we were met by a representative of Nuovo Pignone. He had arranged to take us by train to Florence, where the company had its headquarters.

The day after arriving in Florence we were taken to the Nuovo Pignone plant, a short distance south of Florence. Three representatives of the company and a translator met us to review the draft contract they had previously received. We soon discovered that negotiating with an Italian company was quite different from negotiating with Robert Cort. The Italians proceeded to take each paragraph separately, asking questions about the meaning and suggesting changes. The translator was of great help in the negotiations. He later told us that he had learned English as a prisoner of war in Canada during World War II. At the end of a punishing day we had been able to review the entire contract and agree on changes. They then announced that it was the policy of their parent corporation (one of the Ente Nazionale Idrocarturi group) never to accept a license agreement requiring a minimum royalty for each year, as is customarily required from licensees in the United States.

That evening the prospects for concluding an acceptable agreement seemed remote. We could find only one alternative, which we proposed the next morning. We added up the minimal royalties in our draft and then proposed that this sum be a down payment when the contract was executed. To our surprise this was accepted, and a substantial down payment was made at the time the contract was finalized.

After the trip to Europe, Grove and his accountant, John Collins, began to acquaint themselves with financial details of Walworth and its several affiliates and subsidiaries. They found much that was not to Grove's liking. At one of the board meetings in New York City, Grove spoke very bluntly about certain matters of which he disapproved. He followed this up by instigating a proxy fight for control of the company. Another board member, who also had sold out to Walworth, appeared to support Grove's efforts, but later dropped his support. Since it appeared that Grove could not prevail, he entered into a settlement agreement which provided that Grove would select another member of the board and would be appointed to the Executive Committee together with another member of his choice. In addition, Walworth agreed to a contract by which Grove would receive a royalty on any new line of valves that he might invent.

After settlement of the proxy fight, matters did not run smoothly. Grove invented what he considered to be a new line of valves, referred to as the G5 valve. The board was advised that it would use "O"-ring seals, because this type of seal was well known to the trade. A license agreement for the G5 valve was prepared and submitted to Walworth's general attorney.

During the time that his G5 valve was being developed, Grove became concerned with his holdings of Walworth's stock. The thought was that this asset should be diversified. As a result, a San Francisco broker was retained to liquidate a substantial part of the stock. At that time the opinion among brokers was that the market for Walworth stock was quite thin and that any amount of stock offered for sale would depress the market price. To everyone's surprise, the price actually increased as the stock was offered. Eventually the broker was authorized to sell all the stock, which he did at an average price not far different from the value placed upon the stock at the time of Walworth's acquisition.

At a meeting of the Executive Committee in Houston, Texas, Grove and I announced that the Grove family had sold all of their stock in Walworth, except for a small amount sufficient to qualify as members of the Board and the Executive Committee. We also tendered our resignations from the Board and the Executive Committee. They refused our resignations and requested us to continue on the Board and the Executive Committee and also in our positions with Grove Valve and Regulator Company.

Shortly after sale of the Walworth stock, Walworth's general attorney, who also was a company officer, indicated dissatisfaction with the license agreement. He took the position that, as a Board member, Grove should assign all his inventions to Walworth and should not receive a royalty. As it happened, about the same time financial interests having outstanding loans with Walworth concluded that Walworth needed new management and that Grove would be a good choice for president. With the urging of the financial interests, Grove was elected to this position. However, before he had an opportunity to carry out any of his plans, the financial interests were induced to change their position and Grove and I resigned from all our positions with Walworth, although Grove continued for a short time as president of Grove Valve and Regulator Company. Apparently the financial interests were induced to take the position that Grove should assign his G5 invention to Walworth and should not receive a royalty on its manufacture and sale. Grove flatly refused this demand.

Grove with a Series 600 pipeline valve

Grove resigned from all his positions with Grove Valve and Regulator Company in August, 1960. Following his resignation, Grove filed a court action to resolve his rights with respect to the G5 valve. Walworth contended that the G5 was another version of the Grove "O"-ring-sealed valves. This litigation triggered the filing of other suits by both parties. Eventually the parties agreed to a settlement in which all contracts were terminated, and a substantial payment was made to Grove.

At the time of Grove's resignation from Walworth he was requested to write a report concerning his activities with the company and the company's status. In that report he praised the company's personnel and suggested that John Collins, who at that time was the treasurer of the company, be made president. Walworth followed his suggestion and Collins served as president of the company for many years.

Grove remained inactive for a few years after leaving Walworth. However, manufacturing and the valve business were in his blood and he was not happy about his experiences with Walworth. In 1962 he purchased a small firm in Houston, Texas that was manufacturing what are known as check valves. Not long after that purchase he acquired another small company, Rubber Applicators, which made specialized rubber products for the petroleum industry. These acquisitions gave Grove sufficient space and facilities to develop a new line of fabricated pipeline gate valves. With the help of two employed engineers, he developed a fabricated valve body of novel design, and also a new type of sealing assembly that provided a bubble-tight seal without the use of the "O" ring. Care was taken to avoid any infringement of the Walworth patents on their G4 or G5 valves. The first sales were made in 1963, and about this time Grove moved his operations to a new plant in Houston where, after making some design changes, he proceeded to manufacture and sell the gate valves under the trade name of M & J. The business was incorporated in 1962 under the name of M & J Valve Company. In addition to the large pipeline gate valves, smaller general-purpose gate valves were developed. During the initial years many improvements were made in body design, manufacturing techniques, and seal assemblies. A new building was constructed in 1967 at Satsuma, near Houston, and equipped with machine tools and hoisting equipment adequate for the manufacture of pipeline valves ranging from

12- to 42-inch pipe size and for working pressures ranging from 900 to 1440 psi. Here the company also entered into the system business, including hydraulic valve-operating systems, meter provers, and emergency automatic valve-shutdown systems.

Substantial business was developed by M & J in foreign countries, including the Middle Eastern countries of Iran and Egypt, European countries including England, France, and Holland, and American countries including Canada, Mexico, Venezuela, Argentina, and Brazil.

As the foreign business of the company expanded, it appeared desirable to establish European licensees, particularly in Holland and England. Before establishing a licensee in Holland, Grove attempted to have a shipbuilding company in Holland, Nederlandsche Dok en Scheepsbouw Mij (N.D.S.M.), manufacture the valves according to M & J specifications, and deliver them to a European subsidiary of M & J for distribution to the European and Asian trade. This proved to be unsatisfactory, probably because the Holland shipbuilding company did not have proper facilities for such manufacture, and they did not exercise proper quality control, particularly in connection with their welding operations. Eventually, in place of the manufacturing agreement, M & J granted a license to the company, which permitted the company to sell their product in the European trade.

Another license agreement was entered into with Whessoe in England. Both N.D.S.M. and Whessoe successfully manufactured and sold the M & J fabricated valve.

Over a period of about fifteen years, many inventions were made and patented by M & J Valve. Grove, as president, actively participated in making improvements and developing new products, as inventor or co-inventor with other engineers of M & J. By actual count, seventy United States patents were granted and assigned to the company over this period.

During the latter part of 1976 and early part of 1977 Grove gave serious consideration to a possible sale of his M & J Valve Company. His financial resources were largely involved in the company and the issued stock was in the names of his wife, Julia, and himself. The business was somewhat cyclic, which required financing adequate for slack periods. Several firms made offers that Grove considered unacceptable. Finally a deal was made with Daniel Industries, a firm located in Houston. As of August 2, 1977 Daniel purchased all the issued stock of M & J. Grove agreed to serve as a consultant for a period of one year. As of this writing, the plant is operating in Houston.

The Grove Valve and Regulator Company was sold by Walworth interests that in turn sold the company to Alberta Gas Trunk Lines in 1970. The plant in Emeryville has been retained and is manufacturing essentially the same products as those developed during Grove's ownership.

What conclusions can be drawn from Grove's inventive activities over a period of more than forty years? From the standpoint of social and economic value, his activities are responsible for the creation of two substantial manufacturing firms that have been of unquestionable social and economic value to the San Francisco Bay and the Houston, Texas areas. The products that he brought into being are widely known in the petroleum industry, where they have become valuable in pipe transmission lines, gas and oil production and refining operations. With respect to the U.S. military, many of the products, such as the high-pressure gas and steam regulators and the Flex-flo valves, have become important parts of the equipment of both submarines and surface vessels.

With respect to his status as an inventor, Grove is named as sole or co-inventor in 109 U.S. patents granted over the periods when he was active in Grove Regulator Company and M & J Valve Company. He also demonstrated his ability to organize these companies and, by persistent hard work, to develop them into successful corporations.

William R. Hewlett and David Packard

Electronic Testing Equipment

William R. Hewlett

David Packard

BILL HEWLETT AND DAVE Packard are well known as founders of the Hewlett-Packard Company, which has its main office and plant in Palo Alto, California. Hewlett-Packard (HP) is credited as being the largest and most successful of the many electronic and high-technology companies on the Pacific Coast. Both men are also known for their many activities as individuals. The purpose of this chapter is not to explore their accomplishments in the political, social, and philanthropic fields, but to tell something of the founding of their company and the events that happened in their early years. The period of my work for the company was from the fall of 1939 to the fall of 1946. During the latter part of that period John Swain became my partner; our firm name was Flehr and Swain. During that period Aldo Test also joined the firm as an associate and participated in the preparation and filing of patent applications for HP.

Both Dave and Bill are graduates of Stanford University in Palo Alto, with degrees in electrical engineering. After graduation Bill obtained a Master's degree from Massachusetts Institute of Technology (MIT), while Dave worked for a short time for General Electric. Among others who became well known in the electronic industry, they profited from contact with Frederick Terman, who inspired many Stanford engineering students to create inventions and start new businesses. At the time of my first contact with Bill, my office was in the old Crocker Building located at the corner of Market and Post Streets in San Francisco. Bill had been referred to me as an attorney in the patent field who had had some experience in electronics. During his first visit Bill explained that he had invented a broadband test oscillator that he and David Packard expected to manufacture. He had made the invention some months before and a patent application had already been filed. Later I learned that the oscillator had been the subject of his Master's thesis. Before filing his application Bill had submitted his invention to International Telephone and Telegraph Company (IT&T), probably for an evaluation and to determine what kind of a deal IT&T might offer. Eventually a deal was made in which the legal department of IT&T prepared and filed the U.S. patent application and Bill granted them the right to patent the invention in foreign countries. Bill was to prosecute the application in the United States at his own expense. Following our conference Bill appointed me as his attorney to prosecute the application.

Hewlett (standing) and Packard with audio oscillator in their Palo Alto garage

During the following months I met Dave Packard although I did not visit the so-called "garage" operation where their first products were made. I am told that during good weather assembly was carried out on tables under a large oak tree.

The trade response to the new product was most encouraging. The volume of sales increased rapidly and the pricing provided a good margin of profit. Not many months after their initial manufacturing operations, it was possible to finance their first building on Page Mill Road in Palo Alto. After they located in their new quarters I frequently visited them on patent matters. Bill's function was primarily engineering while Dave was more involved in the financial and business end of the company.

The Hewlett-Packard Company was founded in this garage in Palo Alto in 1939

It is interesting to contrast the financial affairs of the early company with the present-day financing of new companies with venture capital. At all times Bill and Dave were quite conservative on financial matters and their early work was financed primarily by profits.

After being established in their first building Bill took me through the plant and explained their manufacturing operations. Like most electronic products of that time, the broadband oscillator used vacuum-tube circuitry and was assembled from components purchased from various sources. This was years before the days of the transistor or the quartz chip. The components were mounted on a panel and connected by copper wiring. Bill had set up an assembly line that carried out the necessary assembly and wiring operations step by step.

The "redwood building," the first structure built solely for Hewlett-Packard occupancy (1942), with the Navy's excellence flag flying above

From the beginning Bill and Dave had good employee relations. Dave took part in the various activities of the employees, including basketball, which was one of his favorite sports. When they learned that many of the young men had difficulty in financing homes in the Palo Alto area, they were encouraged to organize groups that would take on successive house-building projects on a do-it-yourself basis.

Dave also encouraged the employees to take part in civic affairs in Palo Alto. At that time there was some criticism of the school system, which led to Dave's becoming a member of the Palo Alto School Board. While he enjoyed work on the Board, he was somewhat disappointed in accomplishing only very limited upgrading of the teaching staffs.

With the success of the first product, additional electronic products were developed and marketed. An early trademark registration lists their products as of March 1942 as audio-frequency oscillators, audio-signal generators, and square-wave generators. As of 1946 additional products included voltmeters, frequency monitor and modulation meters, and distortion analyzers. Bill was active in this development work along with other engineering employees. Gradually an organized research and development department was established. A machine shop was created to make parts and components that were not readily available.

Aside from building homes, many of the engineering employees were expert at other do-it-yourself projects. Many did their own automobile repairs on weekends. Dave made the machine shop of the company available for their use and every weekend, weather permitting, a number of the men would work on their cars at the plant and swap auto talk.

On one of my trips from the East back to California, on the old Southern Pacific Streamliner, I happened to meet both Bill and Paul D. V. Manning. Paul had a doctorate degree from California Institute of Technology in chemical engineering. One of us had a compartment where we got together on the second day out from Chicago. Bill and Paul immediately seemed to be attracted to each other and very shortly they engaged in a long discussion ranging from electronics, chemistry, sociology, and politics. I could only be a good listener. Paul later became the Director of Research for International Mineral Company in Chicago.

By the time of World War II the company was making a variety of products, including the original oscillator. Bill enlisted and received a commission. He was stationed in Washington, D.C., where he headed the electronics section of the New Development Division of the War Department Special Staff. Dave, as president, took care of the administrative affairs of the company.

Fortunately a substantial amount of business was maintained that was not for the government. As the war ended Hewlett-Packard, like many of the other California companies, was concerned about the extent to which their business might be reduced. Some of the larger California companies, such as Pacific Gas and

Electric Company (PG&E), had estimated that there would be a dropoff of business of at least 10%, following the end of the war. Fortunately such a dropoff was not experienced by Hewlett-Packard, or by most other California companies. PG&E had to make a quick reappraisal of the situation, and power-generating projects they had expected to postpone were quickly reactivated. Thus it was possible to proceed with further growth and the construction of additional buildings in the Stanford Industrial Park area of Palo Alto.

Early manufacturing activity at Hewlett-Packard

Shortly after the end of the war the Signal Corps of the Army started proceedings to determine whether or not Hewlett-Packard had made excessive profits during the war effort. The company's accountant made a financial report, which was checked by accountants for the Signal Corps. The customary procedure in such matters was for the company to furnish not only its accounting reports, but also a brief explaining the activities of the company during the war effort, the importance of these activities, and any evidence to show that the profits were not excessive. Dave discussed the write up with me, because we had been involved in such proceedings for other clients. I also attended the hearing in San Francisco before the examiners, who had come from the main office in Los Angeles. After Dave made a statement concerning the activities of his company during the war, the nature of the company, etc., the examiners announced what they thought was a fair profit. We were astonished at their decision, which left Hewlett-Packard with very little for the entire war period. They mentioned that if we did not like their decision, the matter might be appealed to the Los Angeles office. After the hearing Dave expressed his disappointment in no uncertain terms. In fact I have never seen Dave as angry as he was at that time. We had no recourse other than to appeal the decision. To our surprise when the matter was presented to one of the examiners in Los Angeles, he seemed to understand the seriousness of the decision on the future of the Hewlett-Packard Company, and as a result he not only restored the sum Dave originally thought would be reasonable, but also allowed an additional amount somehow arrived at with their computations.

Sometime after a number of engineer employees had been hired and were engaged in development of new products, one of the employees came to our firm and explained that he had conceived a new product that he wished to patent and retain for himself. I was surprised, particularly since he indicated that his idea had not been disclosed to the company, and that he did not have a contract requiring him to assign his inventions to the company. I explained that we were attorneys for HP and that I was obligated to advise Packard of the matter. When I later advised Dave of my conversation with the employee, Dave confirmed that it was company policy to not have employee patent agreements with any of the personnel. He explained that it was his philosophy that if an employee was loyal he would disclose and assign any of his inventions to the company. Some years later, when many more employees were engaged in research and development, the company changed its policy and requested all employees to sign an agreement granting HP patent rights to inventions made for the company.

In the chapter about Dr. Bloch I referred to William Hansen, the co-inventor with Bloch of nuclear magnetic resonance equipment. In his search for new products Dave considered the relatively new microwave communication equipment field. He learned that Varian Associates planned to discontinue their work in this field, which William Hansen instigated. About the only tangible thing Varian had left from Hansen's work was a laboratory notebook containing numerous notes, sketches, and calculations. Dave negotiated with Varian for the purchase of this book and after a price had been agreed upon he requested me to prepare a suitable bill of sale. This was an unusual request; laboratory notebooks are seldom sold by themselves. However, I prepared an agreeable document and the deal was consummated. I never knew whether or not the book was of value to Hewlett-Packard, although at about the same time HP began development of a line of microwave test equipment.

Occasionally I became aware of Bill's activities beyond the affairs of the company. He became interested in the environmental problems of Lake Tahoe. One of the organizations, Keep Tahoe Blue, appreciated that the number of beaches available to the public at Lake Tahoe was rapidly decreasing due to sale of beach property in subdivided lots for building purposes. One beach in particular became available for purchase, although the price was such that the environmental organizations could not hope to acquire the property. A California state authority wished to acquire the property but could not act immediately because it lacked proper authority at that time. The owner agreed upon a price that was acceptable but would not hold the property indefinitely pending purchase by the state. Bill somehow learned about this problem and agreed to finance an option for the property with the understanding that the option would later be available to the state authority. Such a deal was actually made, the property was conveyed to the state, and it is now available for public use.

It is understood that as much as half of the total business of the company is now in the computer field. Shortly after the end of the war

Bill came to our office and asked me to make a patent investigation for patents relating to computers. He explained the fundamental basis for all electronic computers, and mentioned certain organizations who probably had patents in that field. We proceeded to make the investigation and reported the results to Bill, with copies of the patents found. It appears that this was probably the start of a research and development project that eventually led to the production of their first pocket-size computer.

Bill Hewlett with one of the pocket-sized calculators that became one of HP's most successful products

It is important for any young company to avoid expensive litigation, such as action for patent infringement. Hewlett and Packard obtained licenses from Western Electric and Radio Corporation of America (RCA), but they were eventually charged with infringement of U.S. Patent 2,133,642 which broadly claimed all crystal-controlled oscillators. The inventor, George Washington Pierce of Harvard University, who was a well-known scientist, filed his first application on February 25, 1924. It disclosed and claimed a communications system including a crystal-controlled oscillator in both the transmitting and receiving stations.

After initial favorable action from the Patent Office, an interference was declared between Pierce's application and two other pending applications that disclosed the oscillator. Pierce's attorney was David Rines of Boston, who prided himself as being an attorney for scientists. Since the interference would delay issuance of a patent for an indefinite period, Rines elected, with the consent of the Patent Office, to file a second application specific to the system, which was not involved in the interference, leaving only the oscillator claims in the first filed application. The second application issued as Patent 1,789,496 dated January 20, 1931. Shortly thereafter it was licensed to American Communications, which paid royalties to Pierce until the patent expired on January 20, 1948. Eventually the interference was decided in favor of Pierce. Patent 2,133,642 dated October 18, 1938 was then issued. Pierce's attorney contended that American Communications should continue payment of royalties for the life of Patent 2,133,642. American Communications refused further payment of royalties on the theory that it was sufficient for them to pay royalty on only the first issued patent since both of the patents were actually based on the same invention, and American Communications were legally bound to pay royalty only for the normal life of a patent monopoly, namely seventeen years. Rines then filed an action against American Communications charging infringement of Patent 2,133,642. The decision of the court, which was sustained on appeal, held that American Communications was required to pay royalty only under the system Patent 1,789,496. Rines then filed an action against Hewlett-Packard for infringement of the oscillator Patent 2,133,642. Our defense of the action, which ultimately prevailed, was that the second patent was invalid since it was based on the same invention as the first patent. Rines unsuccessfully petitioned the U.S. Supreme Court to review the decision.

Although the decision was favorable to Hewlett-Packard, Dave was not happy about the outcome. It was apparent that the situation had been created by the cooperation of the Patent Office in permitting the oscillator per se to be disclosed and claimed in a separate patent. We also were aware of several additional secondary patents issued to Pierce, which were not involved in the litigation, but which might be used as a basis for additional litigation. Dave requested me to visit Rines and endeavor to negotiate an overall settlement that would include a royalty-free nonexclusive license to use any of the secondary patents. Rines was receptive to our offer. He prepared the necessary papers and accepted the payment that Dave had authorized. It was a happy ending for both parties. Today Pierce's invention is used in many systems and products, including watches, microwave communication systems and, in general, a wide variety of electronic circuitry.

Hewlett-Packard did not consider that its products must be protected by patents, although it sought patent protection in instances where the product appeared to have substantial novelty and commercial value. They considered such factors as quality, ease of manufacture, and marketability to be of foremost importance; patents were considered secondary. In other words it was recognized that patent protection on new products was a plus factor, although not essential, and that such protection should not be ignored. This is undoubtedly a rational and practical philosophy for many small companies.

A check of patent records reveals that, over the period from 1939 to 1946, Dave Packard was named as inventor or co-inventor in four U.S. patents, while Bill Hewlett was named as inventor or co-inventor in six.

W. Wesley Hicks and Arthur J. Kercher

Electric Air Heater

W. Wesley Hicks

THIS CHAPTER TELLS THE STORY of two engineers who worked together for many years to develop and market electric air and water heaters. Hicks was an inventor and also the one who commercialized the various developments. Kercher functioned as a consultant who worked with Hicks in inventing and developing many products.

About 1922 Hicks invented an electric air heater (Patent 1,518,007) that became popular for many years, particularly in California. At the time of his invention a widely used portable electric heater consisted of a parabolic metal reflector about fourteen inches in diameter, with a central socket that received a heater element. The heating element was a ceramic core screwed into the socket about which a coiled resistance wire was wound. Many fires were attributed to such heaters. The base to which the reflector was mounted was easily upset to position the reflector face down on a carpet or wooden floor—with obvious results. An additional disadvantage was that the heat was beamed in one direction with the result that someone in the path of the beam might be too warm while those in the rest of the room would remain cold.

Hicks' idea was that an electric room heater should be a permanent part of the wall structure and should heat the air in the room by both radiation and convection, rather than by radiation alone. The heater he invented made use of one or more hollow vertical ceramic cores that carried the coiled resistance wire. The front of the heater housing was covered by a flat grill, and a shell or baffle was located between the ceramic core and the back wall of the outer housing to form a ventilating passage extending from the lower to the upper part of the grill. The arrangement was such that some heat was radiated forward, and by thermal circulation air from the room was caused to flow upward through the core and through the passage between the back wall and the housing, thus heating the air by convection. Because of continuous ventilation, the walls of the outer housing were held at a temperature sufficiently low to avoid any fire hazard. This heater was approved by the insurance underwriters for permanent installation in the wall of a room.

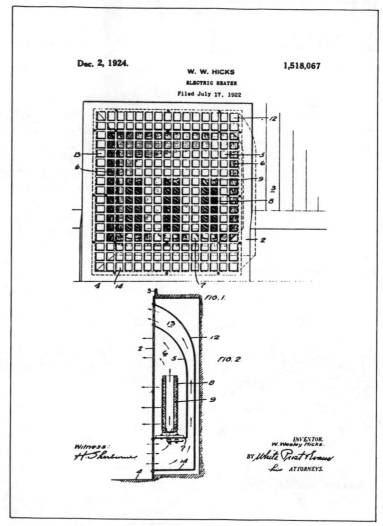

Illustration from one of Hick's early heater patents

Hicks started to manufacture his wall-type heater in the 1920's. It was well received by the trade, particularly by building contractors and architects who liked the idea of permanently installing the heaters in the walls.

Kercher was an outdoor type of German lineage, with a sun-bronzed complexion. He lived in a small cottage in Berkeley, California. His hobbies were fishing and flying. He owned a small single-engine plane which he flew, usually by himself, to his favorite fishing grounds in northern California. I remember one conversation in which he expressed great pleasure at passing his pilot's test at the age of 72. Kercher had a shop in back of his home, where he developed all his inventions. His father was a skilled machinist who could make various parts from Kercher's drawings.

In addition to his wall-type electric air heater, Hicks and Kercher developed an electric water heater for household use (Patents 1,680,622 and 1,671,592). The demand for electric water heaters was limited, although they were used in homes that were completely electrified and in vacation cabins located where gas was not available.

Many of the products developed by Hicks alone and by Hicks with Kercher required specialized thermostatic switches. As the need developed for a particular thermostatic switch, the matter was referred to Kercher, who would develop a switch to serve the required purpose.

For many years Kercher received a royalty from Hicks and his company, and throughout the years of their relationship they remained fast friends.

Not long after commencing the manufacture and sale of his air and water heaters, Hicks recognized that the sale of his products was seriously handicapped by the energy rates being charged by most privately owned utilities. The advent of TVA not only brought this home to him with its low rates but saved the company in the depression years of the early thirties. After extended hearings and arguments with the PG&E officials, Hicks convinced them that it would be in their interest to provide special rates to home users equipped with electric cooking stoves, ovens, and electric air and water heaters. These rate adjustments greatly improved the market for Hicks' products.

At an early date Hicks adopted the trademark Wesix and operated under the name of Wesix Electric Heater Company. Later the firm was incorporated under the same name. From an early date he carried out his business, including manufacturing, in the upper floors

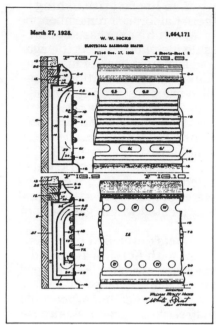

March 27, 1928.   1,664,171

W. W. HICKS

ELECTRICAL BASEBOARD HEATER

Filed Dec. 17, 1925   4 Sheets-Sheet 2

FIG.7.   FIG.8.

FIG.9.   FIG.10.

INVENTOR
WILLIAM WESLEY HICKS
White Prost
ATTORNEYS

Drawing from electrical baseboard heater patent

of the Rialto Building in San Francisco.

Kercher's inventions were not limited to development of products for Hicks. Among others, he developed a motor-driven compressor enclosed in a sealed housing (Patent 1,614,676). I was told that the patent rights on this development were purchased by the General Electric Company.

One product invented by Hicks, and of which he was particularly proud, was his baseboard heater (Patent 1,665,791). Electric heaters built into baseboards were known but were not considered satisfactory. They were fire hazards because the heating element employed was operated at relatively high temperatures. Any cloth object on the floor adjacent to such a baseboard heater created a serious fire hazard. Hicks designed his heating element to form a heated panel surface which operated at a relatively low temperature, below about 180° F.

The business of Wesix not only depended upon the cost of electric energy but also the cost of fuel gas. During the early days of the company, the gas being distributed in California was relatively expensive. Natural gas was available from wells in the Taft area and the San Joaquin Valley, but the available supply did not meet all the needs of the growing population. During the period when gas was relatively expensive, many homes and other buildings with central furnace heating used a semi-refined fuel oil known as stove or diesel oil. A home equipped for oil heating required an exterior tank buried in the ground and a special motor-driven burner which atomized the oil. Although this was a cheap way to heat a home, exterior air pollution was noticeable. Small amounts of polluted air found their way into the home and lodged in draperies, carpets, and upholstery.

A major change in the California fuel situation occurred when natural gas was piped into California from Texas and Oklahoma. This change resulted in a substantial drop in the cost of gas to both homes and commercial establishments.

The business of Wesix was affected by the economic change caused by the influx of low-priced gas. There was no longer an active market for Hicks' water heaters, and home builders ceased to install electric air heaters for major heating. However, his wall heaters continued to be used in bathrooms of new homes and apartments, and also in many new motels.

Hicks had a bad experience in his one and only court action for infringement of his early wall heater patent (1,518,007). During the time his patent was pending in the Patent Office, a friend, William W. Weir, who had been engaged in selling electric water heaters in Seattle, designed a wall-type heater of his own. He showed his design to Hicks, who apparently thought enough of it to refer him to his patent firm, White, Prost and Evans, for filing a patent application. At that time Hicks' application for his wall-type heater was still pending. In due time patents were granted on both applications. However, the claims of the Hicks patent were sufficiently broad to cover the Weir design. Weir refused to acknowledge that his design infringed the claims granted to Hicks. As a result, Wesix filed an action in the Federal District Court for an injunction and an award of damages. The lower court decision was in favor of Hicks, but was reversed on appeal. The Appellate Court pointed to the co-pendency of the two applications in the Patent Office without any interference proceedings to determine which applicant was entitled to a dominating claim. Although Hicks had acted in good faith, he should have advised Weir to obtain his own patent attorney. The Patent Office was partly to blame, too, in that it did not institute interference proceedings to determine which applicant was entitled to priority.

During the post-depression years Hicks initiated a fellowship at Stanford University, under the direction of Dr. Hugh Skilling.

Later, Hicks became concerned over reports from Germany that electric space heaters generated positive ions that were thought to be injurious to health. He promptly encouraged the Stanford fellows that he had established to make measurements of ions from domestic electric room heaters. With their measurement technology he developed a heater that captured any positive ions before they could enter the room. He then funded investigations of the biological effects of negative ions. In the process he developed, with the aid of his chief engineer, Jack Beckett, negative ion generators for use in the home. This research was conducted at Stanford University. The University of California at

Hicks operated in San Francisco under the name Wesix Electric Company

Berkeley and the University of San Francisco proved that ions in the air do have biological effects under controlled conditions but the effects were not significant in ordinary home or office use.

Of the many installations of Wesix heaters in California, Oregon, Washington, and the Tennessee Valley, the most impressive is in the Hearst Castle at San Simeon, California. William Randolph Hearst was fearful of fire, having lost several properties to fires from oil heaters. He believed that Wesix heaters were the safest, and those heaters still operate there today.

After Hicks died the company continued for some time with dwindling business, and eventually it was sold. However, many homes and apartments today have electric wall-type heaters that carry the name Wesix and are still in good operating condition. His story demonstrates how an inventor may build a substantial, profitable business on his inventions, although his products may not be classed as "high technology." One reason why the Wesix Company was successful was because Hicks continuously developed and marketed new and improved products.

Some forty-three patents were granted on the inventions of Hicks or Hicks and Kercher as joint inventors.

Harry E. Kennedy, Lloyd T. Jones, and Maynard A. Rotermund

Submerged Arc Welding

THREE MEN—HARRY E. KENNEDY, Lloyd T. Jones, and Maynard A. Rotermund—made one of the most widely used inventions ever to come out of California. Their patent (2,043,960, granted June 9, 1936) names Rotermund as a joint inventor with Kennedy and Jones, but his participation is unknown to the author. Their welding system, commercialized by the Linde Air Products Company, is now used throughout the world. The circumstances surrounding the making of the invention were unusual, and the basic patent erroneously described the welding method.

In the early thirties Western Pipe and Steel Company, located in South San Francisco, was awarded a contract to supply large-diameter steel pipe for the Hetch-Hetchy water project then being developed by the city of San Francisco to bring water from the Sierra Nevada area to San Francisco. The project included building an aqueduct from the Sierra through the Sacramento River valley, under the southern extension of the San Francisco Bay and then to the foothills for introduction into the spring valley lakes, to form the major part of the San Francisco water supply. The pipe to be made by Western was for penstock use and was constructed from relatively heavy steel plate, which was first bent into a cylinder by machines of the roll type. The longitudinal abutting edges of the plate were then welded together by an automatic welding machine. To prepare the abutting edges for welding, they were bevelled so that an open V was provided for receiving the weld metal. Before using automatic welding, it was customary to apply light tack welding to hold the joint together. The welding head served to feed a welding rod or wire into the joint while it traversed the length of the pipe. The welding rod or wire was coated with a flux material, similar to the flux used to coat welding rods used in hand welding. Usually several passes were required to complete a weld, particularly when the pipe was being made from steel plate of substantial thickness, as, for example, three quarters of an inch or more.

Western Pipe was well equipped with bending and electric welding machines. However, they had never taken a contract to produce large-diameter heavy welded pipe as required by the Hetch-Hetchy project. They sought the advice of Youngstown Sheet and Tube Company in Pittsburgh, Pennsylvania, which had extensive manufacturing facilities for the manufacture of steel pipe. Youngstown suggested a process they had developed and which today is known as "submerged arc welding." This process, known by the name of its inventor, Robinoff, was unique in that a powdered flux was continuously supplied to cover the joint ahead of the welding rod or wire, so that during a welding operation the rod was dragged through the flux. Thus the arc weld took place below the surface of the deposited flux. The flux used by Youngstown was a natural clay that seemed to have the composition necessary for a flux.

While the Robinoff submerged arc process was an improvement over standard arc-welding procedures, it was far from satisfactory. The amount of metal that could be deposited in a single pass was limited, so that in the manufacture of the Hetch-Hetchy pipe it was necessary to make several passes to complete the weld. The process was unstable in that during the welding operation there would be continual explosive effects with discharge of sparks and flux material from the joint. About that time Western contacted the University of California to determine if they had any technical personnel who might be able to improve the process. This brought them in contact with Kennedy, Jones, and Rotermund, who volunteered to see what could be done.

Kennedy and his colleagues appear to have done most of their work in the evening after the Western Pipe plant had shut down. No Western personnel were present during that time, and therefore we can only assume what happened. They undoubtedly noted that after making a weld using the natural clay flux, the flux had melted from the heat of the arc to form a glass silicate that covered the deposited weld metal. It is possible that some of this glass was collected, ground, and then used as a flux. This process would have been some improvement over the use of natural clay. The flux they eventually disclosed was prepared by a mixture of ingredients which when heated to the point of fusion formed a composition that included a substantial percentage of meta silicate. During the course of their research they found that a number of silicates could be used; however, they preferred to use calcium silicate because of its stability at welding temperatures. The required ingredients were fused and then quenched in cold water to form a granular product.

The trio realized that the process they had developed, based on the use of a calcium silicate glass-type flux, was of great value. Accordingly, before discussing the matter with Western, they arranged for a local attorney to file an application for a patent. They then made a disclosure and demonstration to Western without details concerning the flux composition or method of manufacture.

Although Kennedy and his colleagues had done their work on a voluntary basis, without receiving any compensation from Western, Western assumed it was free to use the process and would own any patents that might be granted. Western was disturbed to learn that under the prevailing law they could make no claim to ownership of the invention or patent rights. However, Western continued to maintain that it was free to use the process and to make the calcium-silicate-type flux, despite any patent rights that Kennedy and the others might claim. Accordingly, Western proceeded to set up facilities for making the flux in about the same manner, and to use essentially the same formulation of ingredients.

Three applications were filed in the Patent Office by Kennedy, Jones, and Rotermund over the period immediately following their work with Western. The third application for the first time stated that the invention made use of a new method of operation—namely that the welding current was conducted through the molten conductive flux, and that no arc was

Page from U.S. Patent 2,043,960

present as in conventional welding. The claims in the third application covered the alleged new process, the method of manufacturing the new flux material, and the flux itself as a product of manufacture.

After Western refused to deal with the Kennedy trio on their terms, the latter opened negotiations with Linde Air Products Company, which led to a contract in which Linde agreed to commercialize the process and to pay the inventors a stipulated royalty.

Linde was quite successful in introducing the process for practically all heavy welding operations carried out by machine. Their commercial process was known by the trademark "UNIONMELT." Eventually Western, continuing to use the patented flux, was charged with infringement of Patent 2,043,960 issued on the basis of the Kennedy group's third application. Linde disagreed with Western's contention that it had the right to use the process or, in other words, that it had a shop right to the process. Since Western continued to use the process, Linde brought a patent-infringement action in the Federal Courts. At that time our firm (Flehr and Swain) was brought into the litigation, together with other counsel, to defend the case. Upon reviewing the patent and all possible defenses, it became evident that a technical expert should be retained. In this respect we were fortunate in being able to retain Dr. Leonard Fuller, whom I had known some years earlier as an official of the Federal Telegraph Company. Fuller made a careful study of the process and the patent disclosure. He came to the conclusion that the mode of operation, as described in the patent, was not correct. He then proceeded to set up a series of experiments to demonstrate that in the Kennedy process the welding current was not passing through the molten flux, but actually employed an arc, the same as the standard Robinoff process. In his laboratory work he made several demonstrations to prove his conclusion. The one that, in my opinion, was the cleverest and most convincing was an analysis of voltage wave patterns taken by an oscilloscope. It clearly showed that the wave pattern was that of an arc, and not that of current passing through a conductive material such as molten flux. He also pointed out that the electrical conductivity of the molten flux was such that it could not conduct the heavy weld currents employed.

Fuller's work revealed that the Kennedy trio did have a unique process, but not the one described in their patent. He demonstrated that their process used an electric arc to deposit weld metal, and that the arc was completely enveloped by an envelope of the molten silicate flux while the welding wire traveled through the flux bed.

Fuller's work further suggested that a new flux might be developed, which would not be the same as claimed in the Kennedy patent. He further suggested that we consult with an expert familiar with silicates, namely Dr. Willi M. Cohn. After Cohn became acquainted with the nature of the Linde flux, he developed another type of silicate flux which, in his opinion, would give equivalent results. This flux was tested by Western and found to be satisfactory.

Linde became aware of what was happening and made it known that they were willing to discuss a possible settlement with Western. In the course of conferences between the attorneys, Western's new flux was disclosed, as was the work of Dr. Fuller proving that the mode of operation specified in the patent was not correct. The net result was that a settlement was arranged in which Western was free to continue the use of its new flux, and the action was dismissed.

Following settlement of the litigation against Western, Linde brought suit for infringement against Grover Tank and Manufacturing Company. The defendants in that instance may have become acquainted with the work carried out by Fuller in behalf of Western. Their expert likewise prepared demonstrations to show that the Kennedy process actually used an arc. The lower court in that instance held that the product claims were valid and infringed and that the method claims were based on an erroneous mode of operation and were therefore invalid. On appeal, both the flux and the process claims were held to be valid and infringed. The case was further appealed to the Supreme Court of the United States, which held that the welding product or flux was patentable and that the defendant infringed the flux claims by using an equivalent form of silicate. They reversed the Court of Appeals and followed the District Court's opinion in holding the process claims invalid.

One must conclude that if a corporation requests outside technicians for assistance in solving one of its problems, there should be a clear understanding between the parties with respect to compensation and ownership of patent rights. Further, if claims of a patent are based upon an alleged new process or method, the process should be one that is proven to be correct, and should not be based on speculation. A method based on speculation may be disclosed as such in an application, but not used as a basis for patent claims.

The value of the Kennedy process is beyond estimating. During the war it was widely used in ship-building. It has expedited the manufacture of a wide variety of fabricated steel structures and products, including the large high-pressure fabricated steel valves made by Grove Valve and Regulator Company in Emeryville, California. It is free of all the bad features of the Robinoff process. When in operation it is quiet and free of light flashes and discharge of sparks. Much heavier welding currents can be used, and while it was not practical to use the Robinoff process for welding on steel plates thicker than about one-half inch, the Kennedy process is usable on very heavy steel plate (e.g., two-inch or thicker steel plate). The welds produced are of excellent quality, free from slag inclusions and with a smooth surface. One can truthfully say that the invention revolutionized the automatic electric welding field.

Frederick A. Kolster

Pioneering Electronics Research

THOSE WHO REMEMBER THE earlier radio broadcast days may recall the name "Kolster." The Kolster Radio Company was organized about 1927 as a subsidiary or an affiliate of Federal Telegraph Company. The radio broadcast receiver commercialized by Kolster Radio was known by the trade name "Kolster."

Kolster's experiences in the radio field covered a wide range, including early work as an assistant to Lee de Forest and other wireless pioneers, several years with the U.S. Bureau of Standards, several years in California with the Federal Telegraph Company, and its affiliate Kolster Radio, and then research for IT&T.

Fortunately the Bureau of Standards has supplied me with copies of documents in their files concerning Kolster's early activities before coming to California. One document of particular interest was written by Lloyd Espenschied in May 1942, following a luncheon with Kolster. Documents supplied by IT&T give information concerning issued U.S. patents naming Kolster as sole or joint inventor.

Kolster was born in January 1883, in Geneva, Switzerland. When he was quite young, about two years old, he immigrated with his parents to the United States where the family settled in Boston, Massachusetts. His father was a professional musician and was employed as a violinist with the Boston Symphony Orchestra.

Kolster attended the public schools in Boston and, because he always wanted to be a civil engineer, he attended a manual training high school across the river from Boston in Cambridge, Massachusetts. After graduation he took a position as a surveyor.

One day Kolster received a phone call from his high school principal, who always had taken an interest in him. He said that someone would contact him in connection with taking a position in the new wireless field. He urged

Frederick A. Kolster

Kolster to seriously consider the position as a great opportunity. The person who interviewed Kolster was E. R. Cram, who represented John Stone Stone. Probably Cram had been told by the high school principal that Kolster had unusual capabilities. Kolster accepted the position on condition that he could attend the electrical engineering college of Massachusetts Institute of Technology (MIT). Stone agreed to this arrangement. This was a fortunate decision for Kolster in that it gave him an excellent education at one of the top engineering schools in the United States. He graduated from MIT in 1908.

U.S. Bureau of Standards Radio Laboratory

Kolster worked for John Stone Stone for several years and enjoyed this association. Stone did considerable early work in connection with tuned circuitry for wireless. However, Stone's company eventually failed, leaving Kolster looking for another position.

Kolster then took a position as assistant to Lee de Forest, probably upon the recommendation of Stone. In relating his experiences with de Forest, Kolster referred to de Forest's slap-dash methods of experimentation. Apparently his three-element Audions were being made by another shop in the Boston area. De Forest had a test circuitry in which the Audions were inserted, and if they were noisy or would sing or appear to have some other defect, he would take them out of the test circuit and throw them into a barrel. At that time de Forest was not using high vacuum because it was not attainable with the vacuum pumps available to him.

About 1909 Fritz Lowenstein became president of the De Forest Wireless Telephone

Company. Previously Lowenstein had been Nicola Tesla's right-hand technical man. According to Kolster there was considerable antagonism between Lowenstein and de Forest. De Forest refused to inform Lowenstein of the company's principal activities, including the Audion.

After leaving de Forest in 1911, Kolster took a position with Lowenstein. He recalled that in 1911 Lowenstein was experimenting with Audion circuitry, including circuitry functioning as a sound amplifier. Lowenstein's invention of Audion circuitry used a C battery for the grid bias. Lowenstein was elated to receive $150,000 from AT&T for this invention.

About 1912 Kolster left Lowenstein and took a position in Washington, D.C. with the Bureau of Standards as a radio expert. There he was assigned to carry out technical projects for the Commissioner of Navigation and the Commissioner of Lighthouses. One of his first assignments was to attend the London Wireless Conference of 1912 in the role of a technical advisor to Professor Webster of Clark University. The American delegation to the conference was headed by an Admiral who knew very little about radio but was assisted by Majors Squier, Saltsman, and Russell.

Decremeter set up for operation

To lessen interference between stations, it was decided by the convention that the spark transmitters then prevalent should not exceed a log decrement of 0.2. The Bureau of Standards recognized that this specification could not be enforced in the United States in the absence of practical equipment to measure decrement. The problem of developing such equipment was given to Kolster. As a result, he developed the so-called "Kolster Decremeter."

The Bureau of Standards also credits Kolster with the development of the radio compass (Patent 1,311,654). In this development he made good use of the de Forest Audion, which made possible high detector sensitivity, which in turn made it practical to use small compact-loop antennas. Kolster advocated the marine use of his radio compass with such persistence that the Bureau of Lighthouses agreed to permit installations for test purposes. Three lighthouses were equipped with the compass and certain installations were also made on ships. The success of this test did much to promote the use of marine radio compasses.

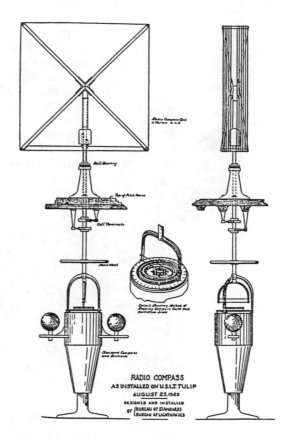

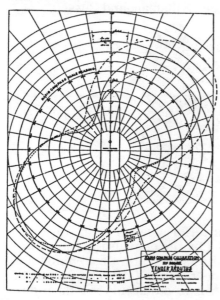

Smith Point lighthouse (above); calibration curve for direction finder on lighthouse tender "Arbitus" (below); radio compass (right)

The Federal Telegraph Company, which was incorporated in California as early as 1912, became aware of Kolster's radio compass and saw the possibility of building a substantial business in the manufacture and sale of radio compasses for shipboard use. They employed Kolster with the understanding that he would carry out further development to produce

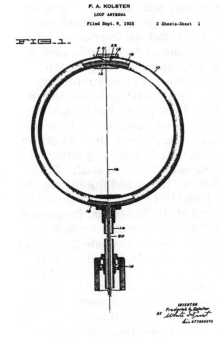

F. A. KOLSTER
LOOP ANTENNA
Filed Sept. 8, 1926   2 Sheets-Sheet 1

FIG.1.

commercial equipment. Further development work was done by Kolster at Federal's laboratory in Palo Alto, near the corner of El Camino Real and University Avenue. A number of improvements of his radio compass were made by Kolster and his associates, including incorporating a deformable cam to make corrections for errors due to nearby magnetic bodies (Patent 1,691,569), and the use of an antenna loop having metal shielding (Patent 1,673,249).

About 1927 Federal and some San Francisco financiers organized Kolster Radio and at that time Kolster took on another project, namely the development of a line of radio broadcast receivers. Although superheterodyne radio receivers were known at that time, they were covered by patent rights owned by RCA and others and were not available for licensing.

Loop antenna (above); illustration from patent for radio receiving system (right)

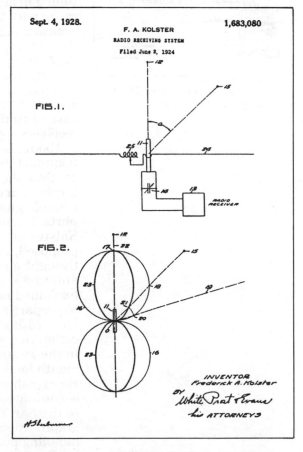

Sept. 4, 1928.   1,683,080
F. A. KOLSTER
RADIO RECEIVING SYSTEM
Filed June 2, 1924

FIG.1.

FIG.2.

INVENTOR
Frederick A. Kolster
BY
White Prost & Evans
his ATTORNEYS

The standard broadcast receiver was of the tuned radio-frequency type, which had several amplifier stages for amplifying the radio signals,

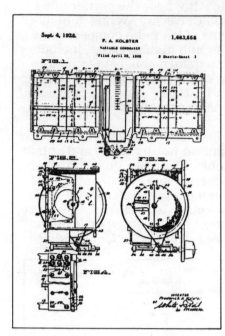

Drawing from Patent 1,683,558 for variable gang condenser

with each stage being tuned by an adjustable condenser or capacitor. Shifting from one station to another was a critical operation requiring precise positioning of the tuning knobs for each tuning condenser. Another inherent characteristic was that the tuning was more critical for the higher than the lower frequencies of the broadcast frequency band.

The receiver developed by Kolster used a so-called gang tuning condenser which adjusted the condensers of all amplifier stages simultaneously with the turning of one knob (Patent 1,683,558). Each variable condenser was also provided with a trim condenser for factory adjustment. Instead of the customary tuning dial, it used a graduated drum that was mounted on the shaft of the condensers. Kolster invented ingenious circuitry (Patent 1,683,081) that made possible tuning in any part of the broadcast frequency range with the same degree of precision and criticality. The radio receivers made by Kolster Radio were of good quality, but their introduction was at a time of severe competition. Shortly after their introduction, the superheterodyne receiver was introduced by RCA and others, and because of their simplicity and ease of tuning, the tuned radio-frequency receivers soon became obsolete.

About the time that Kolster Radio began the manufacture and sale of the Kolster broadcast receiver, there was considerable publicity over airplane accidents due to the absence of reliable guidance systems for the major airports. During one of my visits to Palo Alto, Kolster discussed various systems being proposed, and he disclosed a system that he thought might have merit. He sketched an antenna system that he had in mind and explained how it might be used. He asked me to prepare a patent application covering his idea. Within a few weeks I prepared an application that was approved by Kolster and filed in the Patent Office. During a visit about a month later Kolster was obviously agitated. He explained that a copy of the application, according to customary procedure, was sent to the San Francisco office of Federal Telegraph. Apparently it was seen by someone handling public relations, who reviewed the application and used it as the subject of a press release. According to the newspaper version, Kolster had already invented a new radio guidance system that would make plane landings safer. Kolster's reaction was that as a professional scientist his reputation had been tarnished, since the system was only in the idea stage and its ultimate value was uncertain. His comment was, "They have ruined my reputation as a scientist." Insofar as I am aware the system was never developed beyond the idea stage, although a number of patent applications were filed and issued (e.g., 1,831,011).

About 1927 Federal became interested in the development of commercial radio transmitters and receivers for marine service. In preliminary discussions it became evident that patents owned or controlled by such companies as RCA, AT&T, and General Electric might be infringed, including a number of patents based on inventions of Lee de Forest.

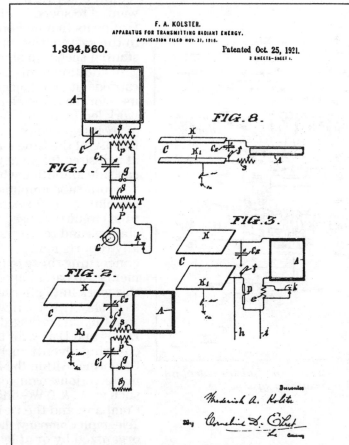

Drawings from early Kolster patent on radio transmitter

As related in the chapter about the Federal Telegraph Company, beginning July 1911, and ending May 1, 1913, de Forest was an

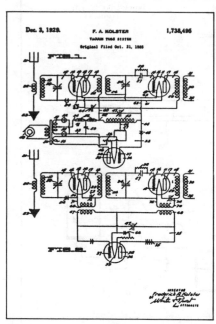

Illustration from Kolster patent on radio receiving system

employee of Federal and carried out considerable experimental work at the company's laboratory in Palo Alto. This was before Kolster was employed there. When de Forest became an employee he signed the usual agreement which required that all inventions he made during the term of his employment would be assigned to the company. One of the projects that de Forest was directed to work on by Federal was the improvement of the radio communications system established by Federal between San Francisco and Los Angeles. Presumably this system made use of the arc generator, a form of transmitter invented by the well-known inventor Poulsen in Denmark, and which had been licensed to Federal. Messages were being sent by the system according to the continental code, which required keying of the transmitter. Federal wanted to speed up the rate of transmission. It appears that de Forest made improvements in the system that indeed resulted in a substantial speed-up of message transmission.

In addition to his assigned work, de Forest carried out experimentation to develop further uses for his three-element vacuum tube. This work led to inventions that later proved to be of great importance. In particular, he developed the use of the tube for generating oscillations at a desired frequency. He also developed the cascade amplifier, which used a number of vacuum-tube amplifier stages connected by coupling transformers. Today such vacuum-tube circuitry is used in all radio transmitting stations and receivers. There is no record of any reports made by de Forest to Federal concerning these experiments and developments. No patent applications were filed on this work until after he resigned from Federal as of May 1, 1913. He then returned to New York City and arranged with his patent counsel, Darby and Darby, for the filing of applications covering inventions he had made while in California. Within the next few years de Forest made various arrangements with companies such as AT&T, Westinghouse, General Electric Company, and the De Forest Telephone and Telegraph Company, the latter being a company organized by or at least controlled by de Forest himself.

In letters exchanged between de Forest and the president of Federal at the time, it appears that Federal purported to release de Forest with respect to any claim it might have to ownership of certain of de Forest's inventions. It also appears that de Forest, in several communications, referred to the "shop rights" of Federal.

Federal in 1924 decided that it should clarify the situation to determine its rights. They requested their San Francisco patent counsel to review all the correspondence and facts, and give them a legal report with respect to their rights. This report was made on October 24, 1924, and relates the facts involved, the legal aspect of the situation, and concludes with the statement that Federal had no claim at that time on ownership of the de Forest inventions. No particular conclusions were made concerning the shop rights which de Forest had mentioned from time to time in their correspondence.

In the latter part of 1925 or the early part of 1926 I was requested to review the October 24, 1924 report and to advise Federal whether or not in my opinion anything could be done at that time. My advice was that I agreed with the findings and conclusions of the report. However, I pointed out that there was necessarily some uncertainty about the situation, because of a recent decision of the Federal Courts with respect to patent assignments, the highly complicated network of contracts that de Forest had entered into since leaving Federal, and the fact that there was no clear understanding as to what the shop rights of Federal might be. The next move decided upon was for officers of Federal to take up this matter with officers of the principal companies involved, namely AT&T, Westinghouse, and General Electric. The net result of such a meeting was that Federal released any claim of ownership that it might have to the de Forest patents, and Federal was granted a nonexclusive royalty-free license under certain of the de Forest patents, including patent rights on the oscillating Audion and cascade amplifier.

Upon reviewing the subject matter of the de Forest patents involved, the engineers of Federal decided that they could develop acceptable radio transmitters and receivers suitable for marine service. Federal then embarked upon a project that extended for a period of several years, and involved the efforts of many engineers, including particularly

Magnetic compass with direction finder attachment

Kolster. Most of the developments centered on equipment operating in the short-wave band, which had been promoted by Fessenden, the great inventor of the continuous wave (CW) and heterodyne systems. Each time a particular circuit was developed experimentally and showed commercial possibilities, it was checked against issued patents to determine possible interference. I performed seemingly endless patent searches and infringement reports.

Shortly after the stock market crash of 1929 it was necessary for Federal to curtail their research activities. International Telegraph and Telephone Company (IT&T) acquired control of the company in 1930, and except for completing some of the work in progress, further work was transferred to the eastern facilities of IT&T in 1931. A considerable number of the employees transferred to IT&T, including Kolster.

For several years I was completely out of contact with Kolster. However, in 1978 we happened to meet on Market Street in San Francisco, close to the old Crocker Building. We immediately recognized each other and stopped to have a brief conversation. He said he had retired from IT&T and was presently living in San Francisco. He said he was writing a book on tuned circuits, and that he would let me have a copy when it was published. During the conversation I mentioned the radio compass that he invented while with Federal (Patent 1,673,249). He said that the invention was being used in all commercial radio compasses. He died within months after that time, presumably with the book unfinished.

My personal feeling is that Kolster is deserving of more credit than he usually gets for his early work on radio compasses, radio broadcast receivers, and commercial transmitters and receivers. The patent records show that he was granted more than 65 U.S. patents in the radio field during the period from about 1919 to 1939. Certainly this entitles him to be classed as a prolific professional inventor as well as a true scientist.

A publication entitled *Radio's 100 Men of Science* by Orrin E. Dunlap, Jr., published by Harper and Brothers, contains biographical narratives concerning 100 men considered important radio scientists. It includes Frederick A. Kolster.

R. G. Le Tourneau

Earth Mover

ALTHOUGH I KNEW LE Tourneau as an inventor and engineer, and as president of R. G. Le Tourneau, Inc., then located in Stockton, California, my relations with him arose out of our firm's representation of one of his competitors, namely Wooldridge Manufacturing Company, located at that time in Sunnyvale, California.

Le Tourneau was an imposing personality, physically large and sturdy but not overweight, and pleasant to all of his friends and acquaintances. He merged religion with all his activities and his honesty was beyond question.

The earth mover, as we know it today, is a bulky wheeled machine that may be pulled by a tractor, or may be self-powered. In operation it moves over a ground area while a cutting blade is lowered to cut through and lift a layer of soil that is delivered into a main load-carrying bowl. One design has the rear wall of the main bowl arranged to slide on a track, so that when it is moved forward the load is expelled over the cutting blade. It also has a front bowl or apron, which is hinged so that it may be raised or lowered relative to the cutting blade. After the main bowl has been filled with soil, the cutting blade is raised and the forward bowl is lowered to retain the load. The machine is then moved to a discharge area where the front bowl is gradually raised and then the load discharged from the main bowl by forward movement of the rear wall. With proper positioning of the front bowl and the cutting blade, the load can be spread as desired over an area that is being filled.

The Le Tourneau invention (Patent 1,963,665), which became known and used worldwide, employed a single winch-operated cable for controlling movement of the rear wall of the main bowl to expel the load and for raising and lowering the front bowl. The reaving of the cable was such that when pulled

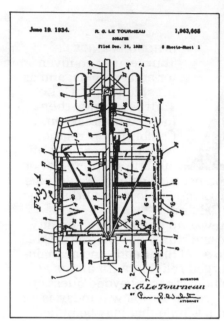

Drawing from Le Tourneau's Patent 1,963,665

by rotation of the winch, the front bowl was first raised relative to the cutting blade, and then the rear wall of the main bowl was moved forward to push the load out of the main bowl. In other words, the single cable made possible sequential operation of the front bowl and the rear wall of the main bowl. The cutting blade was raised or lowered by a separate cable.

Le Tourneau started his business in Stockton as a manufacturer of accessories for Caterpillar tractors, bulldozers, and road scrapers. In the early twenties there was much activity in the Sacramento valley to level farm land for irrigation. This effort led to Le Tourneau's development of a land-leveling machine which was towed over the land by a tractor to move soil from high areas and spread it into lower places. This machine had its limitations, particularly in that it could not move the large amounts of soil required to level quite uneven areas. It was not suitable for road construction work. Subsequently he developed machines (Patents 1,857,157 and 1,891,226) capable of digging and moving larger amounts of soil, but they did not use the single-cable sequential operation described above. The development and manufacture of these machines called for a substantial plant in Stockton, equipped for doing steel fabrication work. At this time and during all his subsequent work, Le Tourneau both headed his company and acted as its chief engineer.

Le Tourneau was unusual in many respects. His academic education probably was limited to high school although it was acknowledged that he had considerable expertise in welding techniques and in fabricating steel mill shapes (e.g., steel plate and structural shapes). His religious convictions were strong and active. Every day all work would stop in the plant at a certain time and he would give the employees a short religious talk. He was a licensed pilot and used his private plane to attend various religious meetings in other cities.

The introduction of Le Tourneau's earth mover, as described above, met with wide commercial success. The combination of the large load-carrying bowl together with the forward bowl or apron made for good load-carrying capacity, together with controlled discharge of the load over a desired area. The single-cable control with sequential operation of the expeller of the main bowl and the front bowl was relatively simple; it permitted the use of a single winch for controlling the cable, and it provided the advantage of automatic sequential operation of the main and forward bowls. The machine was adaptable to a variety of projects, such as road building, dam construction and land leveling. Sales increased rapidly and soon required more adequate plant capacity. About 1945 Le Tourneau established a second plant in Peoria, Illinois, which eventually became his main plant.

As generally happens with most successful inventions, commercial success brought competition from several sources. One competitor was the Wooldridge Manufacturing Company, Inc., which our firm represented. Another competitor was the Gar Wood Company. Neither Wooldridge nor Gar Wood used a sliding expeller for discharging the load from the main bowl. Instead, the bottom wall of their main bowl was hinged so that it could be swung upward and forward to discharge the load. They both used a single operating cable reaved in such a manner as to produce the sequential operation explained above.

About 1941 or 1942 Le Tourneau filed an action in the Federal Courts charging Gar Wood with infringement of Patent 1,963,665. The principal evidence offered by the defendant to show that the patent was invalid was Le Tourneau's own Patent 1,891,266, which did not have the single-cable feature, and Patent 1,174,834, which disclosed the idea of moving two loads sequentially by use of a single cable. Mainly on the basis of this evidence, the lower court held that the patent was invalid, and the decision was upheld on appeal.

Some time after final determination of the suit against Gar Wood, the Le Tourneau Patent 1,963,065 was reissued (Re. 22,783, August 27, 1946) by the Patent Office, with somewhat modified claims. The Patent Office file of the reissue application revealed that a representation had been made to the effect that the court's decision was based upon certain technicalities, and that the court did not make a decision that would invalidate the modified reissue claims. In 1947, almost immediately after granting of the reissue patent, Le Tourneau filed an infringement action against Wooldridge. Our law firm at that time, Flehr and Swain, was served with a copy of the complaint about noon of the day in which it was filed in San Francisco. We concluded that it would be better for Wooldridge to have any action of this kind pending before the same judge who made the decision in the Le Tourneau/Gar Wood litigation. This meant that the action should be filed in Sacramento where this judge (Judge Lemmon) was presiding. We quickly prepared a complaint for declaratory relief. John Swain then drove to Sacramento and was able to file the complaint on the same day. Subsequently the attorneys for Le Tourneau agreed to permit the case to remain in Sacramento before Judge Lemmon.

Shortly after filing the action against Wooldridge, we proceeded with discovery to learn more information about the circumstances surrounding the reissue patent. To our surprise we learned that following the decision in the Gar Wood case, one of the attorneys for Gar Wood approached Le Tourneau's attorney and proposed to cooperate in reissuing Le Tourneau's patent. He proposed that he would prepare the reissue documents and carry out prosecution before the Patent Office at the expense of Gar Wood. Gar Wood was to obtain some benefits from this arrangement, particularly a nonexclusive royalty-free license to any reissue patent that might be granted. Shortly after learning about this most unusual arrangement, we proceeded to take the testimony of some of the attorneys involved and also the deposition of Le Tourneau himself.

Le Tourneau in his deposition was almost painfully honest. He virtually confirmed that the lower court in the Gar Wood case was correct in its reasoning that incorporating the special cable for sequential operation of the expeller of the main bowl and of the front bowl did not amount to invention and was within the skill of an ordinary engineer familiar with these mechanisms. At the conclusion of his deposition he spoke to everyone of the group and shook hands with a smile.

Toward the end of the discovery period we prepared and filed an amended complaint, which not only asserted that the reissue patent was invalid but in addition charged antitrust violation on the grounds that the plaintiff was trying to enforce his reissue patent against the industry well-knowing that it was invalid. Gar Wood was also made a party defendant.

The next highly unusual event that occurred was a demonstration made in the Southern

California desert near Palm Springs. We received a notice stating that a deposition would be taken at that place on a specified date, the deponent to be the expert for Gar Wood. When we arrived at the designated place, we found a huge truck elaborately equipped with camera and sound equipment in preparation for a demonstration of one of the Gar Wood machines. They started the camera and sound equipment while the technical expert made a speech concerning the machine, and then proceeded to show how the machine was operated. Unfortunately a diesel engine on the tractor made considerable noise, and the earth mover was also noisy in operation, with numerous squeaks and squawks. Along with all of this a court reporter was endeavoring to record what was said by the expert and the questions being asked by the attorney. We objected to this extravagant demonstration, pointing out that we had no forewarning of what was going to take place, but there was nothing we could do except to watch the proceedings.

At the conclusion of the demonstration, which took a couple of hours, I stated that we should have the right of cross-examination with the film equipment. Gar Wood's attorney announced that he would be glad to make the equipment available to us for cross-examination purposes, but that this would be at the expense of Wooldridge. He indicated that this expense would be about $10,000 a day. Since it was late in the afternoon I again repeated the demand that we be given the right of cross-examination, together with the equipment, beginning the next morning.

When we arrived the next morning the equipment was gone and their excuse was that we had not made an arrangement for its retention. However, the technical expert and reporter were present, and we proceeded to interrogate the expert. This, of course, was quite unsatisfactory, although during the interrogation he admitted that the soil being handled during the demonstration was not typical since it was mainly desert sand.

About two months after the desert demonstration we were requested to come to Los Angeles to review the film and sound track taken during the demonstration. When they ran the film, it was apparent that much had been deleted and that the spoken part varied

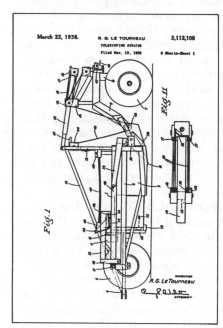

March 22, 1938. R. G. LE TOURNEAU 2,112,105

TELESCOPING SCRAPER

Filed Nov. 10, 1936 6 Sheets-Sheet 1

Fig.11

Fig.1

INVENTOR
R. G. LeTourneau

ATTORNEY

*Telescoping scraper — one of
Le Tourneau's further
improvements in earth-moving
equipment*

considerably from the stenographic version. Consequently, I refused to stipulate introduction of the film as evidence, much to the disappointment of Gar Wood's attorney. Not long after this fiasco, I was advised that both parties wished to settle. We worked out a simple settlement that was approved by both parties. Wooldridge was granted the free right to continue manufacture and sale of their earth movers and received some payment from Le Tourneau.

In addition to his original earth-mover invention, Le Tourneau made other inventions, particularly improvements in the related earth-mover items. His company built earth movers of various sizes and capacities, which were pulled by tractors of suitable sizes. Le Tourneau recognized that there was a practical limit to the size of such machines, which led him to develop self-powered earth movers. They were driven by diesel engines and required special steering arrangements capable of resisting severe shocks, since the machine had to be capable of traveling over rough ground. These machines were made in sizes capable of taking on loads of eighty yards or more. They were capable of traveling at speeds much greater than earth movers pulled by tractors. On large projects these machines proved to be more economical and generally superior to smaller tractor-drawn machines.

Le Tourneau was continually striving to produce bigger and better machines. He conceived that instead of driving the machine by use of conventional transmission and differential to the back wheels, an ideal large earth mover would be one in which power would be applied individually to each of the four wheels. This led to a long and difficult project to develop an electric system that included a diesel engine driving a direct current generator, an electric motor geared to each one of the four wheels, and an electric controlling system. Since no available electric motors were suitable for this purpose, Le Tourneau attempted to design a new motor within his own organization. The operating requirements for the motors was such that most engineers would have said the project was impossible. In addition to considering compactness and horsepower, it was evident that the motors would require an effective cooling system to prevent overheating. Further, it was necessary that the motors cope with dusty conditions that are generally present during operation of earth movers. Any dust finding its way into a motor might well cause clogging. After struggling for some time over the motor problem, Le Tourneau engaged the help of Westinghouse Electric Corporation; after considerable work by Westinghouse engineers, suitable motors were designed and manufactured. Finally, Le Tourneau was able to market a fully electric machine.

Le Tourneau eventually sold his earth-mover business to Westinghouse. This may have been the end result of the extensive assistance that Westinghouse had given him in the design of the new motors. Le Tourneau then went to Longview, Texas, where he built a plant for the manufacture of various fabricated steel products, especially offshore drilling platforms. By coincidence I visited Longview during the building of his plant, but I did not have any contact with his company. However, there was much talk among the engineers in Longview about how the plant was being constructed by Le Tourneau's employees, using Le Tourneau's welding techniques. One of Le Tourneau's fabrication specialties was the use of box beams in place of ordinary mill shapes such as I-beams, channels, and the like. Box beams were also used on his earth movers, giving his machines a distinctive appearance.

Le Tourneau is an example of a person who was a successful inventor as well as a general engineer and businessman. His earth-mover inventions revolutionized large scale soil-moving operations and are now considered essential for projects such as dams, canals, and highways.

Charles W. Merrill

Gold Recovery from Cyanide Solutions

CHARLES WASHINGTION MERRILL made a spectacular success promoting an invention that he made shortly after graduating from the College of Mining of the University of California at Berkeley, in 1891.

During the latter part of his college days he had become interested in the alkyl cyanide process for recovering gold from ores. He directed his college thesis to a description and analysis of this process. At that time the process was not being used to any extent in the United States, but was used in a limited way in South Africa. According to the practice in South Africa, the gold content of crushed ore was leached out by a solution of sodium cyanide and then precipitated by flow of the solution through a box containing zinc chips. A fair amount of the gold was precipitated on the surfaces of the zinc chips, which were then smelted to recover the gold. The general consensus of the mining industry was that the process was inefficient and left much to be desired.

By the late 1800's the U.S. gold-mining industry had undergone notable changes. Much of the gold mining in the years immediately following the 1849 Gold Rush was carried out by individuals or small mining companies, but by the late 1800's much of the mining was in the hands of companies of substantial size.

After his graduation in 1891 Merrill lost no time in getting a position as assistant to a well-known San Francisco mining engineer, Alexis Janin. This position gave him the opportunity to use Janin's laboratory facilities for his own purposes. It was during his association with Janin that they filed an application for patent on a cyanide process (U.S. Patent 515,148) which, however, did not disclose the process that Merrill later developed. He left Janin in 1893 and opened his own office in San Francisco. His first engagement was with

Charles W. Merrill

Standard Consolidated Mine at Bodie, California. At present Bodie is a ghost town of interest to tourists. I visited Bodie about 1940 and at that time it comprised a number of unattended empty houses and stores, and an old-fashioned cemetery with a decrepit funeral hearse. Empty coffins, large and small, were strewn about the cemetery. The ore-processing mill was one of the largest structures of the town. We were told that it was still being worked by a few employees, but at a fraction of its capacity. Like many mill buildings, it was stair-stepped up the side of a mountain so that material being processed moved downward by gravity. Merrill spent about a year and a half at Bodie to prove out his process, first on an experimental pilot-plant basis, and then on a full-scale commercial operation.

UNITED STATES PATENT OFFICE.

ALEXIS JANIN AND CHARLES W. MERRILL, OF SAN FRANCISCO, CALIFORNIA.

PROCESS OF LEACHING ORES WITH SOLUTIONS OF ALKALINE CYANIDES.

SPECIFICATION forming part of Letters Patent No. 515,148, dated February 20, 1894.

Application filed June 12, 1893. Serial No. 477,338. (No specimens.)

To all whom it may concern:

Be it known that we, ALEXIS JANIN and CHARLES W. MERRILL, citizens of the United States, residing in the city and county of San
5 Francisco, State of California, have invented an Improvement in Processes of Leaching Ores with Solutions of Alkaline Cyanides; and we hereby declare the following to be a full, clear, and exact description of the same.
10 Our invention relates to an improvement in the art of leaching ores with solutions of alkaline cyanides and consists in, first, precipitating and separating, in the form of silver sulphide, by means of an alk—

generated will also combine with the free alkali to form an alkaline cyanide. 50

We have found that, whereas silver is not precipitated at all, or only very imperfectly from strong solutions of potassium cyanide, by means of the agents hereinafter mentioned, yet when the silver bearing solution contains 55 only about one and one-half per cent., or less of pure potassium cyanide (K C N) or its equivalent, then the silver can be thoroughly precipitated by means of the sulphides of sodium, potassium or ammonium, or by sul- 60 phureted hydrogen gas, and the precipitated silver becomes more imperfect as

---

Merrill took on the Bodie project as an opportunity to prove out details of the improved cyanide process that he had in mind. His deal with the company was that he would not take any pay until, and unless, the process was a success. At the conclusion of the project, Bodie conceded that the process was very much a success. There is no record of the compensation that Merrill received from this project, but undoubtedly it was substantial. Merrill had no investment in the project other than his time, since Bodie paid for all the equipment required.

The process that Merrill installed for Bodie differed in several respects from the cyanide process practiced in South Africa. As the gold-precipitating agent he used zinc powder, which he termed "zinc dust," rather than zinc chips as in South Africa. Crushed ore solids were treated with an alkyl cyanide solution, to dissolve the gold content. The solids were removed from the cyanide solution by filtration. Zinc dust was intermixed with the cyanide solution, and the solution then supplied to a filter of the leaf type. Precipitated gold and also some unreacted zinc dust were deposited on the leaves of the filter and as feeding of the solution to the filter continued, some further precipitation took place between the unreacted zinc dust on the filter leaves and the cyanide solution. The solution was then recycled to treat additional batches of ore. The gold on the filter leaves was then recovered by smelting.

Before the ore was treated by cyanide solution, the major part of the gold content had been removed by other methods. One such method was to cause crushed ore solids to contact mercury to form a gold/mercury amalgam. The ore solids remaining after such preliminary treatment were commonly referred to as "tailings." Many of the mills discharged their tailings on an outdoor stack, in the hope that someone would eventually develop an efficient process for removing the remaining gold content. Merrill's process was well-suited for that use and made possible the recovery of 85% or more of the gold previously left in the tailings.

The work that Merrill did at Bodie was not simply to substitute zinc dust for zinc chips. Analytical laboratory work was required to determine the gold content of the tailings and whether they contained ore materials that would inhibit subsequent precipitation. If so, preliminary treatment was required to remove the inhibiting factors. It was also necessary to develop effective means for introducing and dispersing a controlled amount of zinc dust in the cyanide solution. The zinc dust had to be introduced in such amounts as to provide an optimum amount for efficient precipitation. The leaf filter for receiving and collecting the precipitate was somewhat critical with respect to timing of the precipitation cycle, to provide optimum deposition on the filter leaves without obtaining deposits that would require excessive pressure drop across the leaves. It appears that Merrill's one-man operation resolved all these matters and provided a complete system of equipment designed to carry out his process.

Merrill's next project was at the Harqua Hala mine in Arizona. Based on the experience that he had gained at Bodie, he first arranged an experimental pilot-plant operation, and after the success of that he engineered a commercial operation. His work at the Harqua Hala mine was in 1894 and 1895.

Following his success at the Harqua Hala mine Merrill was approached by the English owners of the Montana Mining Company, whose mine was located at Marysville, Montana. Preliminary laboratory analysis confirmed his opinion that his process could be used with advantage by the Montana mine. As with Bodie and Harqua Hala, he promised a preliminary experimental installation. This proved to be highly successful and led to the construction, under his supervision, of a commercial plant. After the commercial plant was brought into successful operation, he continued to manage and supervise the operation for about two years as Resident Metallurgical Engineer. He quit this position in 1898 and returned to San Francisco, although he was retained as a consultant by the mine for another two years.

No records appear to be available concerning the compensation Merrill received from any of these projects, except that they were on the basis of "doesn't work, no pay." Nowadays very few inventors would risk years of their services in the hope that fair compensation would be negotiated if the invention worked to the satisfaction of the client. However, Merrill was dealing with savings in gold of known value. The overhead factors could be readily determined, and although no actual figures are known, a large mine might experience annual savings in thousands of dollars by recovering most of the gold in its tailings. Merrill undoubtedly understood the value of his plant installations and probably received ample

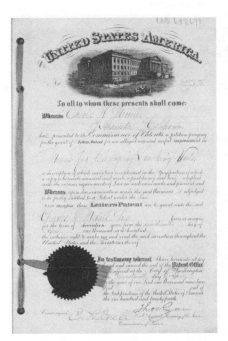

Facsimile of one of first patents issued to Charles W. Merrill—U.S. Patent 647,678, April 17, 1900

compensation. It also appears that well before 1900 Merrill had filed several applications for patents, and the compensation that he received undoubtedly included a substantial amount for a license to use his inventions.

His next project, started in 1898, was with the Homestake Mine in Lead, South Dakota. Homestake resulted from the consolidation of several smaller mining claims, engineered by George Hearst and his associates. As early as 1880 Homestake's operation was producing more than one million dollars in gold annually. The basic process of the mine as of 1898 was said to be use of mercury to extract gold from the crushed ore. However, they probably also used equipment known at that time, such as jigs and classifiers. The use of mercury was generally in connection with sluice boxes. In their normal operations, about 75% of the gold content was recovered and the remainder was lost in the tailings. The solids of the tailings comprised sand, together with extremely fine clay solids commonly referred to as "slimes." The sand could be readily separated from the slime solids, but the slime solids were difficult to remove from a slurry. The Homestake engineers initially suggested that the Merrill precipitation process might be used in one phase of their process, but after considering their proposal and making some preliminary laboratory tests, Merrill convinced them that his process was not suitable for that usage. During his study of Homestake's entire process, he noted that much gold was being lost in the slime solids of the tailings. He convinced Homestake that an experimental plant should be constructed to try out application of his zinc dust/cyanide process to the tailings. As carried out in the experimental plant, the tailings were treated for removal of the sand content, and the slime slurry fraction was dewatered in a slime filter. The dewatered slime solids were dispersed in a sodium cyanide solution to dissolve out the gold content. The slime solids were removed from the cyanide solution in a filter of the leaf type, after which zinc dust was intermixed in controlled amounts with the clarified solution, and the solution fed to a precipitating leaf filter, where the precipitated gold was deposited on the filter leaves. At least in some instances the filter cake in the slime filter press was aerated to oxidize certain ingredients that interfered with efficient precipitation. Here again it was necessary to adapt the process to the nature of the specific ores being processed and to develop suitable equipment for the system.

Merrill slime filter in Homestake Mining Company plant at Lead, South Dakota (top); original Homestake slime plant at Deadwood, South Dakota (bottom)

Based on successful operation of the experimental plant, Homestake agreed to build a commercial plant under Merrill's supervision, which would have a capacity adequate for their mill. Eventually this was completed and put into successful operation.

With respect to his compensation, Merrill made a somewhat better deal with Homestake than with the mines where his process had previously been installed. Homestake agreed that for a ten-year period he would be paid a definite percentage of gold recovered by his process. No records are available as to exactly how much money was paid to Merrill under this contract, but obviously it was a relatively large sum and what at that time would be considered a fortune. Merrill stayed with Homestake during the ten years of his contract, probably to make sure that his process was kept in continuous and efficient operation. During the period of the contract, Merrill hired a number of young mining engineers, including particularly Charles C. Broadwater, Louis D. Mills, and Frank H. Ricker. Broadwater was a graduate of the Royal School of Mines, Mills was a graduate of Stanford University in mining and metallurgy, and Ricker graduated in mechanical engineering from Iowa State College. It is not clear if they were employees or shared in the project, but in any event when Merrill subsequently organized a corporation for commercializing his process and equipment, all three became members of his organization.

Merrill's wife remained with him while he was at Lead and it was there that three of his five children were born. After returning to the Bay region he established his residence in Berkeley, where he built a home in which he lived for many years.

The success of Merrill's precipitation process became widely known throughout the United States and foreign countries. A considerable demand was created for his process and the equipment he had developed. He appreciated the opportunity to establish a substantial business in the licensing of his process and the sale of the equipment required. To take care of this business, he organized a California corporation in 1910 under the name of Merrill Metallurgical Company. Not long after incorporation the name was changed to the Merrill Company. Merrill was president, and Broadwater, Mills, and Ricker were officers and directors. A friend of Merrill's, Herbert Shuey, joined the organization in its early days and became vice president. Lou Mills became active in promoting commercial sale of the Merrill process and equipment in foreign countries. He was also an inventor and developed a number of improvements to the process and equipment. In dealing with particular firms, the Merrill Company was able to supply specialized equipment to carry out the process, together with specific instruction for its installation and operation, and license rights under the Merrill patents. Each transaction required a sales contract and a separate license agreement. Since gold and silver mines throughout the world became aware of the Merrill precipitation process as early as 1908, particularly by way of articles concerning the process appearing in mining journals, the demand for the equipment and process continued for many years.

The Merrill Company did not have facilities for manufacturing the equipment involved. Some of the auxilary equipment was available from various manufacturers in the United States and foreign countries. Specialized equipment, specifically adapted for use with the Merrill equipment and usually covered by patent rights, was either manufactured for Merrill by subcontractors in the San Francisco Bay region, or made by the mines from drawings and specifications supplied by Merrill.

Part of the Merrill Company's exhibit at the Panama-Pacific International Exposition in San Francisco, 1915

In the early days before the Merrill Company was organized, it was necessary to import zinc dust from a Belgian company. With expanding business it was necessary to find other sources of supply. In 1916 Minton H. Newell, a chemical engineer, joined the Merrill Company. He had developed a new process and equipment for manufacturing zinc dust. The Merrill Company formed a separate subsidiary, known as the Alloys Company, to produce zinc dust according to Newell's process. Merrill financed the building of a plant, which then became a principal source of supply of zinc dust for mining interests throughout the world. The market for zinc dust expanded into other fields, and the company eventually developed a variety of zinc-dust products having different specifications to suit particular industries. The Alloys Company was sold to the Metals Disintegrating Company, of Elizabeth, New Jersey, in 1945.

In 1915 the Merrill Company had an exhibit at the Panama-Pacific International Exposition in San Francisco. The exhibit included a typical installation of the Merrill process.

The part played by Herbert Hoover during World War I as U.S. Food Administrator is well known. Not so well known is the part played by Merrill. Immediately after Hoover accepted the position of U.S. Food Administrator, he contacted Merrill to head the division of Collateral Commodities. Merrill accepted this position on a no-salary basis. He served in this position under Hoover in Washington, D.C. until the end of the war in 1918. During that time the Merrill Company was left in the hands of Charles Broadwater, Herbert Shuey, Lou Mills, and Frank Ricker. Merrill enjoyed his work under Hoover and felt that he had really done something for the war effort.

The business of the Merrill Company gradually tapered off after 1918. Many mines could not operate profitably because of high operating costs and the declining price of gold. Since Merrill had adequate capital, he considered the possibility of developing inventions made by other parties. The first invention in which he became interested was a valve invented by Sven J. Nordstrom, a Swedish mining engineer. The original Nordstrom patent is U.S. 1,180,312, which was granted on an application filed in the Patent Office on November 2, 1915 and issued April 25, 1916. The chapter of this book on Nordstrom relates the circumstances that led to this invention.

Charles Merrill organized the Merco Nordstrom Valve Company, to which Nordstrom assigned his invention. In general the company was a success, although it required consid-

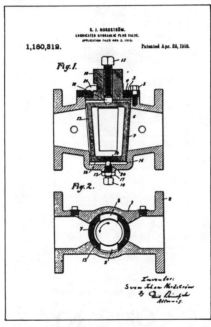

Drawing from patent for Nordstrom's lubricated plug valve

erably more capitalization than Merrill had originally anticipated, mainly because of the expensive metal-working equipment required to make the valves. About 1932 the Merco Nordstrom Valve Company was sold to Rockwell Industries.

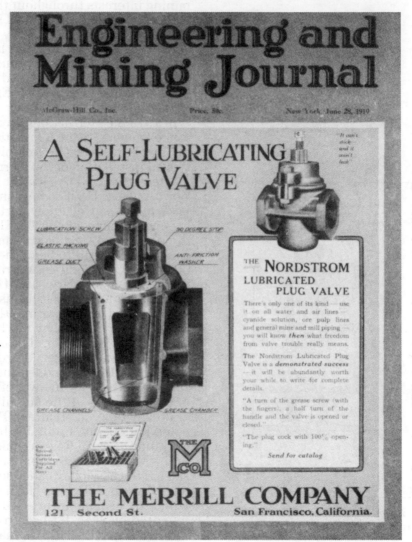

One of the first advertisements for the Nordstrom lubricated plug valve, June 28, 1919

Thomas B. Crowe, a metallurgical engineer, was employed by the Merrill Company shortly after the end of World War I. Lou Mills and Crowe became great friends and spent much time together, both being avid fishermen. Not long after Crowe became an employee it became evident to Merrill that his cyanide process could be improved if he had a simple way to remove air from the solution before introducing the zinc dust. A number of methods were proposed to accomplish this de-aeration, but they either were too expensive or did not work. When Tom Crowe became aware of the problem, he immediately suggested that there was a very simple way to accomplish the desired result. His solution was to introduce the cyanide solution into a vertical tank equipped with baffles so that solution introduced into the upper part of the tank would cascade down over the baffles to the lower end, and then be removed. The tank would be continuously evacuated to maintain an adequate partial vacuum to cause most of the absorbed air to be removed. The solution would be removed from the bottom of the tank by a suction pump which would operate against the vacuum within the tank. The solution would be admitted to the upper part of the tank under control to permit maintenance of the desired partial vacuum. Crowe's proposal was immediately tried out experimentally and found to be workable and to de-aerate the solution to such an extent that the precipitation of the gold from the solution by adding zinc dust was greatly improved. Merrill, when he learned of Tom's invention, recognized that it was of considerable value to the company, and instead of immediately requesting that Tom assign patent rights to the firm, he treated him as if he were an independent inventor. He advised Tom that the invention was of value to the company, and that he wished to have the subject matter patented and, assuming that Tom was willing to assign it to the company, he wished to pay a reasonable royalty for use of the invention. Tom, in his self-effacing manner, replied that he doubted if the invention was patentable and in any event he saw no reason why he should get anything extra and was quite willing to assign it to the company. Merrill refused to accept that, and as a result the company paid for filing a patent application, and a contract was entered into between the company and Tom in which the company agreed to pay a royalty for exclusive rights under the patent, for its life. A patent application was filed on March I7, 1917 and issued as Patent 1,321,986 on November 18, 1919. Tom remained with the company for many years, until his death.

He received the royalty until the patent expired in 1936. The Merrill process with his de-aeration feature became known as the Merrill-Crowe process.

Harrison S. Coe, a mechanical engineer, retired about 1929 after many years with the Dorr Company in Stamford, Connecticut. While with the Dorr Company he had done extensive work in connection with hydraulic separators such as are used in the mining industry, and in preparing mathematical tables used by engineers in designing equipment in that field. He established residence in Palo Alto, California, with his daughter. Having considerable time on his hands, he started the development of some of his ideas. One was a centrifuge, suitable for the mining industry, which would operate continuously on mining slurries without clogging. He built a small centrifuge and tested it in part of the old structure in Palo Alto near University Avenue and El Camino Real which at one time was occupied by the Federal Telegraph Company. His centrifuge prevented clogging by recirculating a certain amount of the discharged material back through the peripheral discharge nozzles. On the basis of his laboratory work, he submitted his drawings and centrifuge to the Merrill Company with the thought that the company, with its connections to the mining industry, would be an ideal organization to commercialize the invention. Merrill and Lou Mills were impressed with the centrifuge and they made an arrangement with Coe for undertaking manufacture and sale. At that time Coe had not filed application for patent. They suggested that Coe take his invention to the firm with which I was associated at that time, for preparing and filing an application. The work was delegated to me, and on the basis of Coe's description and drawings, a preliminary draft was prepared and sent to Coe for his approval. Coe was pleased with my efforts and within a short period some revisions were made and the application filed in March 1930.

Unknown to Coe or me, additional applications were pending in the Patent Office at that time, all containing broad claims to the same general subject matter. The Patent Office declared an interference between Coe, a party by the name of Albert Peltzer, and an application assigned to the De Laval Company. An interference proceeding was initiated by the

Coe's centrifuge

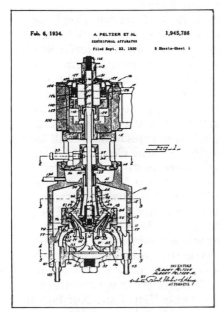

Peltzer's centrifuge

Patent Office to resolve the question as to which one of the parties was the first inventor and entitled to a patent containing the claims involved. During the preliminary period of the proceedings, De Laval brought a motion to terminate the interference on the basis of an earlier disclosure they had located. Although this disposed of the interference, it left serious questions with respect to the relationship between Coe's centrifuge and that of Peltzer.

With Merrill's authorization, I retained a private investigator in Chicago to contact Peltzer and determine his attitude toward granting rights to commercialize his centrifuge. In due time the investigator made his report, which said that Peltzer was quite willing to discuss granting a license or otherwise making a deal to commercialize his invention, and that his employer, Corn Products Company in Chicago, had released him so that he was free to deal with other parties. Merrill's only comment with respect to the investigator's report was to express regret that the investigator had seen fit to feed drinks to Peltzer to obtain all the information for his report. In any event, Peltzer, at the request of Merrill, came to California in 1930 and made a deal with the Merrill Company to commercialize his invention, along with the invention of Coe. The two centrifuges were actually not competitive, in that Coe's centrifuge was suitable for the mining industry, whereas Peltzer anticipated the use of his invention in the starch industry. However, features in Coe's centrifuge were used to improve the Peltzer machine.

The net result of the negotiations with Coe and Peltzer was that the Merrill Company organized a new affiliated corporation called the Merco Centrifugal Company. A more complete story about Peltzer appears later in this chapter.

My work on the Coe patent application led to a meeting with Louis D. Mills, who at that time was taking care of patent matters for the Merrill Company. My office was in the old Crocker Building on Market Street, directly across from the Palace Hotel. It had survived the 1906 earthquake and had retained some old-fashioned customs. One was that each office room had a handsome brass spittoon that was kept in top-notch condition. I had relegated mine to a corner of the room where it was not noticeable. On the occasion of Lou

Mill's first visit, before being seated he looked around the room and finally asked, "Where is your spittoon?" I retrieved it and Lou placed it by his side where it was used occasionally during our meeting. I was careful to have it available for future visits. This episode should not lead one to believe that Lou was a rough character. Actually he was a professional engineer of absolute honesty.

Following my work for Harrison Coe I was requested to handle the patent work for the Merrill Company and also for the Merco Nordstrom Valve Company. Up to that time the patent work for these companies had been handled by a New York attorney, Archibald Cox, the father of the Archibald Cox who became well known as an investigator in the Watergate fiasco. It was typical of Merrill that instead of abruptly advising Cox that I was to handle future patent matters for his companies, he arranged for Lou Mills, Nordstrom, and me to visit Cox in New York to arrange for the transfer. We traveled on the old Forty-Niner train, which preceded the streamliners. The locomotive was a coal burner and fine cinders filtered in on the vestibules, making for a crunching sound when one walked from one car to another. The dining car was Southern Pacific's best, with excellent food. Nordstrom proved to be a gourmet and soon became a friend of the head steward in the diner.

Our visit with Archibald Cox, whose office was in the Woolworth Building, was very pleasant. During the same trip we called on Alexander Neave, Sr., since it was anticipated that his firm (Fish, Richardson & Neave) might be retained in connection with patent-infringement litigation for the Merco Nordstrom Valve Company.

Peltzer, while with Corn Products, had built a small demonstrating centrifuge, which he brought with him to California. Before attempting to commercialize either the Coe or Peltzer machines, laboratory tests were carried out and both machines were improved. Peltzer's machine not only employed continuous return of material to prevent clogging but also introduced wash water with the return. It was evident that Peltzer was thoroughly acquainted with the wet starch process then in use by Corn Products and other starch companies in the United States. One feature of the standard wet starch process was the use of tables for the separation of starch from the gluten. The tables were shallow troughs made of wood and generally about 110 feet long and divided into 10 channels, each about 2 feet wide, with a slope of about 5 inches from the feed end to the discharge end. A slurry containing starch and gluten, termed "mill starch," was fed at a controlled rate to the upper feed end of a table, to produce an even flow distributed as sheets over the surface of the troughs. During the flow, starch settled out from the gluten to form a starch layer over the table surfaces, and the gluten was discharged at the lower end of the table. After the starch layer reached a certain depth, the flow was stopped and the starch layer removed by hand shoveling. Depending upon the capacity required, a mill would employ several such tables. Being made of wood, they were subject to deterioration and had to be rebuilt about every 20 to 30 years, at great expense. Peltzer firmly believed that his centrifuge could be used in place of tables for this primary separating step. He also believed that his centrifuge could be used for many other separating operations in the over-all milling process. Before Peltzer developed his centrifuge there had been many attempts to use centrifuges in connection with the starch process. However, they were crude devices incapable of making a sharp separation between starch and gluten.

About that time Clarence Brown, a graduate engineer from Massachusetts Institute of Technology, became an employee of Merco Centrifugal and was assigned to assist Peltzer in making a series of demonstrations at one of the Corn Products starch plants. In preparing for the demonstration, Peltzer was careful to make complete records of the various methods he wished to try. Applications were prepared and filed in the Patent Office, covering all these methods. The earliest of these applications was filed January 14, 1933.

Corn Products consented to the demonstrations and permitted Peltzer to try out his centrifuge for several separating operations in the wet starch process, including its use in place of tables for the primary separating operation between starch and gluten. During the demonstration, Peltzer was in continual communication with engineers of Corn Products, and Corn Products was fully appraised of all the various tests being made at locations in the plant process where separating operations were required. Peltzer thought the demonstration had gone very well. However, to his surprise, Corn Products announced that they were not interested in purchasing the Peltzer centrifuge, because they did not believe it would materially improve their process. They also mentioned that during Peltzer's demonstrations they had made a number of changes in their process to improve its efficiency.

After Peltzer returned to California, it was decided to demonstrate the machine to other starch manufacturers who used the wet starch process. They had some initial success with A. E. Staley Company, who purchased machines they used for recovering starch from gluten tailings. Staley was impressed with the machines and pleased with their operation, but at that time they did not proceed to use the machines for other operations.

Not long after the demonstration with Corn Products, we became aware of a number of patents being issued to Corn Products on the basis of applications filed after the Peltzer demonstrations. It was clear that although the Peltzer process applications were filed at an earlier date, the Patent Office had failed to set up an interference between Peltzer and the Corn Products patents, to determine who was the first inventor. In contacting other companies in an effort to sell the Peltzer machine, Clarence Brown had been advised that they did not wish to purchase machines until it was determined whether Corn Products or Merco Centrifugal would obtain dominant patent rights.

With the authorization of Charles Merrill, we proceeded to have the Patent Office set up interference proceedings between the applications of Peltzer and the conflicting patents of Corn Products. Interference proceedings were also instigated between Peltzer and some pending applications of Corn Products of which we became aware. The net result was several different interferences, each of which was of considerable importance.

Interference proceedings in the Patent Office as of that time, and even up to the present, are tedious and lengthy and frequently take several years to conclude. Fortunately the Patent Office consented to consolidate a number of the interferences for the purpose of taking testimony. The decision in such proceedings is based upon the depositions of witnesses for each party and pertinent documents (e.g., sketches and descriptions) that they identified. In preparing for taking depositions Clarence Brown was of great help in locating various documents and preparing witnesses.

Fortunately, the final decisions of the Patent Office in all the interferences were in favor of Peltzer. To the credit of Corn Products they let it be known to the trade that the interferences had been decided in favor of Merco Centrifugal and that there was no longer any question about whether Corn Products or Merco Centrifugal would dominate this field. Not long after final decisions in the interferences, patents on the Peltzer applications involved were issued. The most important patent, 2,323,077, contained claims covering the Peltzer machine at various places in the wet starch process, including primary separation between starch and gluten.

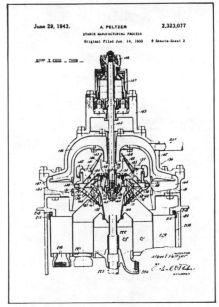

Drawings from Peltzer's Patent 2,323,077 (starch manufacturing process)

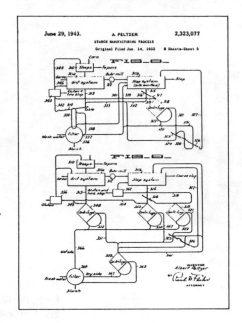

By coincidence, the starch tables of a number of the larger starch manufacturing companies were due to be replaced. It was obviously good judgment to acquire the Peltzer centrifuge and discontinue entirely the use of starch tables. Thus, since there was no longer any question of possible domination by Corn Products, all the starch companies, including Corn Products, became interested in purchasing the Merco centrifuge. Although World War II interfered with many anticipated sales, after the war Merco Centrifugal enjoyed a thriving business manufacturing and selling the Peltzer machine. Component parts of the machine, such as the stainless steel bowls, required special techniques for proper machining. This work, together with other component parts of the machines, was done by subcontractors, with Merco Centrifugal doing the final assembling and testing.

Merco centrifuges operating in a large starch plant

Following the acquisition of Merco Nordstrom Valve Company by Rockwell Industries in 1932, Merrill decided to dispose of Merco Centrifugal. In 1956 the company was acquired by Dorr-Oliver, which at this writing is manufacturing the centrifuges in its plant at Stamford, Connecticut. Since initial introduction to the starch industry, the machines have been found useful in many other industries where separations must be carried out continuously and the feed material contains undissolved solids.

David D. Peebles

Instant Dry Milk Powder

David D. Peebles

DAVID PEEBLES IS WELL known by the dairy industry for both his inventions and his business activities over a period of more than fifty years. He is credited with more than 200 U.S. patents, mainly in the dairy and food-processing industries.

One of Dave's outstanding characteristics was his unlimited enthusiasm for various sports and hobbies, in addition to his interest in developing new processes and products in the dairy and food industries. An avid outdoor sportsman, every year he took time off for hunting and fishing. Another one of his hobbies was raising and training bird dogs.

Of the various inventions that he made, the most important and well known is instant dry milk powder.

One can easily find various brands of dry milk powder on the shelves of a supermarket, but the products are all essentially the same. When added to cold water they quickly dissolve and form a stable reconstituted liquid milk. It is hard to realize that prior to 1947 such a commercial product did not exist. What was sold as a dry milk powder was quite difficult to disperse in cold water. When added to a tumbler of cold water it would float on the surface, and when one attempted to disperse it by vigorous stirring, it would form sticky lumps. The only practical way to reconstitute such a powder with cold water was to use a motor-driven mechanical mixer. Such milk powder was produced by spray drying, and its use was largely confined to the commercial baking and ice cream industries, where mechanical mixers were normally employed.

Another notable but less known invention made by Dave was a method for producing a stable dry whey powder that would not cake when exposed to the atmosphere. Before that invention most whey, produced in the manufacture of cheese, was fed to pigs or discharged into the nearest stream. Peebles' invention made it possible to sell the whey powder in cloth or other non-moisture-proof bags without the troublesome caking.

Dave's father and mother first migrated to Utah, probably during the early part of this century. His father established a small mission in Utah, but the mission did not prosper and the family then came to Eureka, California, where Dave was raised. His education was gained in the Eureka public schools. According to my recollection, he mentioned receiving a nontechnical college degree. Dave was interested in pursuing a career as an opera singer and received some voice training. He came to San Francisco hoping to further his ambition, but had no success except for some recitals at the old Palace Hotel. One would hardly expect a person of such background to eventually become a successful inventor and businessman.

After forgoing his opera aspirations, Dave took a position as an apprentice with a steel fabricating company, Union Iron Works, in Oakland. Among other things, they manufactured a variety of equipment for the marine trade, including stills and evaporators. The knowledge that Dave obtained on that job was used to good advantage in his later work.

Probably about 1918, Dave returned to Eureka. He had developed a growth on his vocal cords. The growth was removed by surgery and, although he recovered physically, his singing voice was ruined.

In Eureka he formed a partnership with Fred S. Bair, George T. Tooby, and Frank H. Tooby, which was known by the name of Bair, Peebles, and Tooby. At that time the dairy interests were important in Eureka, and it appears that the purpose of the partnership was to commercialize equipment and processes for the dairy trade. The records show that Dave was granted patent 1,438,502 dated December 12, 1922 for "Method of Concentrating Liquids Containing Organic Matter." The application on which the patent was based was filed October 30, 1918. Although this early patent was assigned to the partnership, subsequent applications filed in the early twenties were not so assigned and were granted in the name of Peebles himself.

In 1928 Dave became interested in the

development of spray dryers suitable for producing dry milk powder. His first patent on a spray dryer (1,830,174) was filed January 31, 1927. An application for an improved dryer was filed July 16, 1928 and granted June 20, 1933 as 1,014,895.

In 1928 Dave became interested in developing commercial products from the whey produced by cheese manufacturers. He organized a new company, Western Condensing Company, about 1928, the purpose being to develop salable new products made primarily from cheese. About 1938 Western Condensing Company acquired a plant in Appleton, Wisconsin, on the Fox River. The plan was to develop products using the whey produced in large quantities by the Wisconsin cheese industry. Initially the two main products were the previously mentioned stabilized dried whey powder and dry lactose (i.e., milk sugar). The Wisconsin organization was under the management of Reginald (Reg) Meade, Dave's son-in-law, a graduate chemical engineer. Reg organized a group of more than forty graduate engineers who did creditable work in exploring and developing new whey processes and products, including fermentation processes and products (such as riboflavin), pelletized whey products and processes for extracting and refining lactose from whey. Reg himself is named as inventor or co-inventor on fourteen U.S. patents pertaining to milk and whey processing and products.

During the early years of Western Condensing, Dave negotiated an agreement to license certain patents of his to Golden State Milk Company. He also made some improvements in the Grey Jensen spray-drying equipment, which Golden State had widely licensed to the dairy industry.

In his early work Dave probably felt the need of basic chemical knowledge. In 1931 he became associated with Paul D. V. Manning, a young graduate chemical engineer with a Ph.D. degree from the California Institute of Technology (CalTech). Paul was interested in research and he admired Dave's creativity. Their first work together was to develop an improved method for cooking fish (Patent 2,060,232) for the F. E. Booth Company. The method they developed, which cooked the fish (pilchards) in open cans and at controlled humidity, was quite successful. For the succeeding years until about 1941 Paul continued to work with Dave on various projects and was named with Dave as a joint inventor in ten U.S. patents. During that time Paul also was a consultant to Marine Magnesium Company, a struggling young company in South San Francisco producing magnesium hydroxide and other magnesium products by precipitation from sea water. Probably Paul's greatest value to Dave was the chemical knowledge, in which Dave was lacking. Paul particularly gave him a better understanding about the protein of dairy products, and the effect of milk processing on the protein content.

Western Condensing had very meager research facilities in Petaluma, California. They used a rundown wooden building along the Petaluma slough as a place where equipment and methods could be tested. They also had a small chemical laboratory in the main office building. One employee in particular, Paul Clarey, was of great help to Dave in trying out different ideas. Dave could tell him about an idea during a short conference or over the telephone, and Paul would try it out the next day. Present-day research groups would frown on such shortcut and "cheap" research, but it produced results.

With respect to his invention of stable whey powder, which preceded the instant milk, Dave realized that a commercial market for whey could not be developed for a product in liquid or concentrated form. Fermenting organisms in whey resulting from cheese manufacture made storage in liquid or concentrated form impractical, aside from the expense of marketing in bulk or in containers. The spray dryers that he developed using a centrifugal atomizer (U.S. Patents 1,830,174; 1,914,895; 2,574,705; 2,473,035) as normally operated, produced an anhydrous powder that was hygroscopic and subject to caking when exposed to the atmosphere. He reasoned that if the lactose content could be converted to crystalline form (alpha monohydrate), the powder would be nonhygroscopic and stable. In his experiments a quantity of anhydrous spray-dried whey powder was exposed to the atmosphere and permitted to form a cake. The powder produced by grinding such a cake was relatively nonhygroscopic and stable. The problem was to find a commercially practicable and inexpensive process for producing such powder. To that end Dave arranged a drum that was rotated about its axis. A batch of anhydrous spray-dried whey powder placed within the rotating drum was slowly moistened by a fine water spray. By controlling the amount of moisture added, with rotation to continuously agitate the batch, some of the lactose content was crystallized to produce a powder that was relatively stable.

Dave filed a patent application on his rotating-drum process. He soon learned that applications by other inventors were also pending in the Patent Office, all describing various processes for making similar whey products. The Patent Office instigated an interference proceeding to determine which one of several applicants was the first inventor. Two of the applications were assigned to, or allegedly owned by, the Kraft Company. Kraft filed a motion to dissolve the interference, charging that the broad product claims were unpatentable over earlier disclosures. This was conceded by Dave and the interference was terminated. In the meantime Dave developed what he considered to be a more practicable process (Patent 1,928,135). For a time this process was used commercially but it was not the final answer. Early in 1936 Dave, jointly with Paul Manning, invented the simplified process of Patent 2,088,606, in which concentrated whey was spray-dried, using a Peebles centrifugal atomizer, and the drying conditions were controlled in such a manner that the product leaving the dryer had sufficient moisture content to convert the lactose to the monohydrate crystalline form. After leaving the spray dryer, the moist powder was further processed to reduce its moisture content. This new process met with instant commercial success. Kraft recognized its merits and negotiated a license. The process is still being used for producing stable dry whey products from cheese whey or so-called "modified whey" from which certain ingredients have been removed.

Peebles wanted to manufacture lactose as well as stable dried whey. Together with Thomas Marquis as a co-inventor, he developed a process for producing a partially refined crystalline lactose (Patent 2,439,612).

During World War II penicillin was in great demand. The prevailing process for its manufacture employed a fermentation broth containing various nutrients. Lactose was found to be a good nutrient for this purpose. By the end of the war Western Condensing was supplying about 80% of the lactose used in the United States for this purpose.

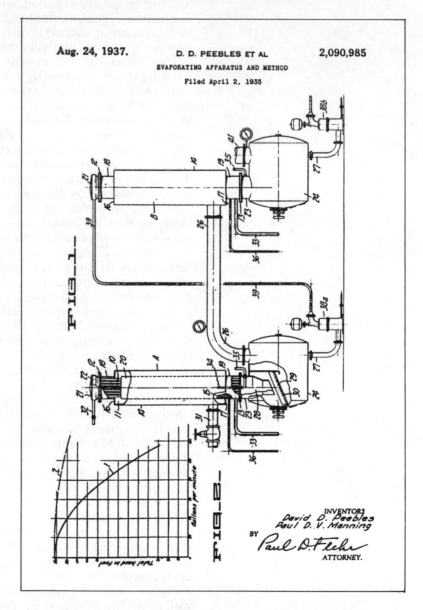

Aug. 24, 1937. D. D. PEEBLES ET AL 2,090,985

EVAPORATING APPARATUS AND METHOD

Filed April 2, 1935

FIG._1_

FIG._2_

INVENTORS
David D. Peebles
Paul D. V. Manning
BY
Paul D. Fleh
ATTORNEY.

Dave, in conjunction with Paul Manning, invented an improved vacuum evaporator (Patent 2,090,985) which today is well known and still used in many processing operations. It is of the tubular type and generally known as the "Peebles high-velocity down-draft evaporator." Features of the evaporator are that the amount of liquid present in an evaporating stage is relatively small, and the dwell time in each stage is relatively short. These features, together with efficient evaporation, made the evaporator useful for evaporation of various liquid materials where it is desirable to minimize time/temperature factors.

After the end of World War II, Dave acquired a small farm at Davis, California where he was close to the Davis branch of the University of California. Before that time he had gone through the trying experience of divorce and remarriage. His second wife, Margaret, was an enthusiastic equestrienne. The farm had a stable where Dave kept the horses. At the request of certain of his friends on the teaching staff of the university, he gave lectures to the students in the Dairy Department and was awarded an honorary doctoral degree.

For many years Dave dreamed and frequently talked about the need for a dry milk powder that could be easily dispersed in cold water to make a good quality reconstituted milk. He had learned much from Paul Manning about protein chemistry and the effect of denaturing the protein content. He knew that the protein content of a good quality spray-dried milk powder was relatively undenatured, because of the temperature/time factors of the processing treatment before and during spray drying. During his previous work on whey he had attempted to use similar processing on nonfat milk (skim milk) without success.

His initial idea leading to instant dry milk was to apply lactose syrup to particles of nonfat spray-dried milk, the thought being that the applied lactose would make the milk particles more wettable without denaturing the protein, so that the product could be more readily dispersed in water. He phoned Paul Clarey from Davis and requested him to try out the idea. The next day Paul rigged test equipment consisting of a spray-dryer chamber having a lower conical part and an upper part connected with air inlet pipes. He used a paint spray gun to produce atomized droplets of lactose syrup. Then anhydrous nonfat dry milk powder was fed into the inlet air stream so that the powder was dispersed in the dryer chamber and discharged from the lower end. As later explained by Paul, he placed a plastic sheet on the floor below the dryer chamber and then, lying on his back, he held the spray gun so that the atomized lactose syrup was discharged upward through the bottom outlet and into the chamber, where it intermixed with the dispersed powder. To his surprise the material coming out of the chamber looked like snow flakes. He collected a fair batch of the material on the plastic sheet and then took it to the laboratory, where he made some simple tests. He found that when added to cold water in a tumbler, it wet and sank immediately. A little stirring with a spoon was sufficient to produce a complete dispersion. He phoned Dave and explained what he had done. Since it appeared that the product had considerable moisture, he placed the sheet with the product on a hot air register, thinking that the product should be dried out. Dave came to Petaluma the next day and noted that although the product was highly wettable and dispersed readily in cold water, the resulting milk was not stable because the heat treatment on the hot air register had denatured the protein. When the reconstituted milk was permitted to stand, undesirable sediment collected on the bottom of the vessel.

During the days following the first experiment, it was determined that water could be used in place of the lactose syrup. It was also found that if final drying were carried out so that the protein was not appreciably denatured, the product had the desired property of forming a stable reconstituted milk that would not settle out.

Dave thought he should gain more information about the temperature/time factors for final drying, before designing a plant for commercial production. He delegated Thomas Marquis to carry out a research project to obtain data for guidance in preparing for commercial production. Marquis' work clearly showed that final drying could be carried out within certain time/temperature values without appreciable protein denaturing.

Dave then assigned the job of designing prototype commercial equipment to Paul Clarey. Within a few months Paul had collected and assembled the necessary components of a complete system, and was able to demonstrate that the system was suitable for commercial manufacture.

In my preparation of a patent application to cover the process, it was explained to Dave that we should know with certainty why the product was highly wettable and dispersible in cold water. Since several different theories had been advanced, the matter was submitted to Stanford Research Institute (SRI). After studying the method and making some experiments, the SRI experts concluded that the instant properties were due to the structure of the granules, namely that the granules were made up of spray-dried particles bonded together in the form of porous agglomerates. This was disclosed in the application which issued as Patent 2,835,586.

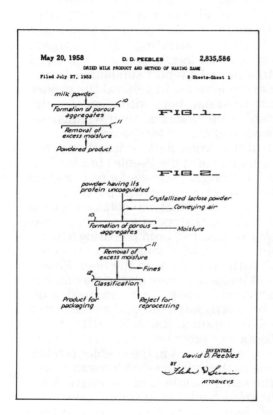

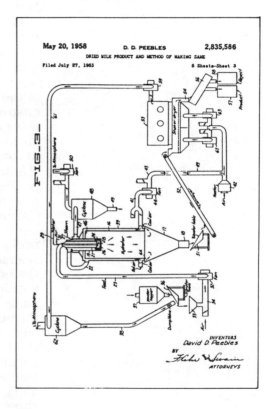

During the time the patent application was pending, there were considerable differences of opinion among the Western Condensing officials about how to commercialize the product. Western Condensing had no experience in consumer marketing and their estimates of the capital requirements for manufacturing and marketing the instant milk product were staggering. Some thought that customers would not pay a premium price for the product, but such a price appeared necessary to cover the additional processing and equipment expense. To settle this question, arrangements were made for trial marketing under the supervision of a well-known advertising firm of Batten, Barton, Durstine, and Osborne.

Sacramento was selected as the area for the trial marketing. A prototype manufacturing unit was set up in Tulare, California, under the control of Tom Marquis. The product was packaged in cardboard cartons with blue labeling bearing the name "Peebles Instant Milk." Advertising was limited to local newspapers and emphasized that the product was instantly dispersible in cold water by stirring with a spoon to provide liquid milk of beverage quality. During the marketing period, customers were contacted for their appraisals. At the end of the trial period a report summarized the customers' reactions. In general the report was quite favorable, both with respect to the customers' evaluations and their willingness to pay a premium price for the product.

Some of the larger milk-processing companies took notice of the Peebles Instant Milk product, and bought packages for examination. Carnation Milk Company was particularly interested in the product and obtained several packages. By coincidence Carnation, at considerable expense, had been preparing to enter the nonfat spray-dried milk market in competition with other firms in the field. Final plans and budgeting were on the agenda for the next board meeting, which was held at the end of, or shortly after, the trial marketing of the Peebles product. Ralph R. Brubacher, Carnation's vice president in charge of sales, had become interested in the Peebles product and came to the meeting with a package to show the other members of the board. He brought along a pitcher of water and some drinking glasses and proceeded to demonstrate how the product would produce a stable reconstituted milk by simply adding it to the cold water and stirring with a spoon. The board members, including the president, Eldridge H. Stuart, were greatly impressed. They agreed unanimously to drop plans for their conventional spray-dried product and start negotiations with Western Condensing to obtain the exclusive right to manufacture the Peebles product.

Carnation promptly revealed its interest to Dave and proposed a plan for commercial production. Briefly, the plan involved incorporating a new company to be known as Instant Milk Company, to which the patent rights would be assigned. The stock of the new company was to be divided between Western and Carnation. The new company was to undertake the manufacture of the product, and Carnation would provide the capital necessary to establish commercial manufacturing facilities and to properly introduce and market the product to the consumer trade. In addition, Western Condensing would receive a royalty based on the product sold by Carnation. After drafting and executing the necessary contracts, Carnation immediately proceeded to set up the necessary facilities for manufacture and packaging, and within a relatively short time the product was introduced to the market.

Carnation's commercial efforts were tremendously successful. They prepared several facilities for commercial manufacture, designed new labeling bearing the trade name Carnation, made deliveries to the trade and ran extensive advertising in newspapers and on television. Their George Burns and Gracie Allen television shows were popular events and carried highly effective advertising. In the first marketing period (July 1954 - March 1955), Carnation instant dried milk captured about 16.4% of the total national consumer market for nonfat dry milk powder. In the second marketing period (March 1955 - March 1956) it captured 29.8% of the national market. By 1958 it was difficult to find any of the old spray-dried product in supermarkets. In addition to these rapid increases in the early years following its introduction, the total amount of dry milk powder sold in the consumer trade, particularly after licensing, increased dramatically.

Although he recognized the commercial success of the product and had received an honorary award for the invention, Dave was not particularly happy about the commercial outlook for Western Condensing Company, Instant Milk Company, or for himself. He was particularly disappointed in Western's share of royalties from Instant Milk Company. Another factor was a proxy fight by some dissatisfied stockholders of Western who wanted to gain control of the company. Eventually in 1956 Western was merged with Foremost Dairies. Dave was given the title of Assistant to the President and Director of New Products and Research at Petaluma. However, Foremost research was carried out within rigid formal procedures while Dave was prone to "short-cut research." On April 16, 1961 Dave resigned his positions with Foremost.

Much of the activity just described, including the introduction of Carnation into the picture and their commercial activity, occurred while the patent application was pending in the Patent Office. Prosecution of the patent application did not proceed without difficulty. Initially it was filed with claims to the method, the apparatus, and the product. Eventually claims to the method were allowed but claims to the product were rejected. Claims to the apparatus were subsequently transferred to a separate application. On appeal to the Patent Office Board of Appeals, the rejection of the product claims was affirmed. An appeal was then taken to the District Court of the District of Columbia. Judge Pine presided at the trial. During my opening statement he indicated displeasure when I mentioned that the commercial product was nonfat milk powder. Apparently he considered that fat was an essential ingredient of any milk.

During the first day of the court's session I used Dave as a witness to explain his own invention. I was disturbed by some of his responses, which did not seem to be consistent with the questions. Later Dave said that he had neglected to use his hearing aid! Some enlarged microphotos were produced during Dave's testimony. The judge asked if it was necessary to look through a microscope to find the difference between the claimed product and the prior ones. The judge also refused to admit into evidence a small bag containing a sample of typical common spray-dried milk powder. He said that we should submit an unopened commercial package. After the session we visited several markets to locate such a package. Most of them stocked only nonfat dried milk of the instant type. Finally we found a store that had one old package, which the judge accepted the next day.

During the second day's session I used Doctor Julius MacIntire as an expert witness. He is highly educated and at that time headed that part of Carnation's research department in Los Angeles dealing with milk processing and products. The judge was obviously impressed with MacIntire and his testimony. At one point he took over the examination. By the end of the day he had decided that the product was patentable.

Dave's discontent with what he considered to be a lack of adequate benefits from Instant Milk Company to Western led to negotiations that resulted in sale of Western's interest in Instant Milk Company, to Carnation. The settlement included assignment of the patent rights to Carnation. However, after acquisition of Western by Foremost Dairies, a new deal was made between Foremost and Carnation in which the Peebles/Carnation patent rights, as well as certain patent rights of Foremost that were considered to be conflicting, were assigned to a new company known as Dairy Foods Incorporated. The primary function of Dairy Foods was to license the combined patent rights to the dairy industry.

After Dave's resignation from Foremost Dairies he became a consultant to Carnation. His propensity for invention was still with him and while with Carnation he developed high-speed equipment and methods for "instantizing" milk and other food products.

Some time after Dave's death in 1965, Carnation disposed of its stock interest in Dairy Foods to a Canadian corporation that was affiliated with Foremost-McKesson, Inc., being a consolidation of Foremost Dairies and McKesson. Licensing activities were continued and by 1971 the major dried-milk producers in the United States were licensed and paying royalties to Dairy Foods. Firms in England and France were also licensed under corresponding foreign patents.

As generally happens with patents on valuable inventions, a number of infringements occurred in the United States, England, and France. The ensuing litigation extended over several years, but in all instances the defendants settled by taking licenses.

Dave is named as inventor or co-inventor in more than seventy U.S. patents in the dairy field, plus many in other fields. The total economic impact of his inventions is difficult to evaluate, but obvious effects can be summarized as follows. Within a few years following the trial marketing of Peebles Instant Milk to the consumer trade, the dry milk industry was completely revolutionized and the old spray-dried milk powder for the consumer trade became obsolete. This involved a dramatic change in the manufacturing operations of the industry, requiring new processing equipment and new marketing techniques. The consumption of dried nonfat milk powder in the Unites States increased rapidly after introduction of the Peebles product, which is attributed to the consumers' immediate appreciation of its merits. The success of instant dry milk stimulated development of many other "instantized" food products. The equipment, methods, and products developed have varied with the food involved. One might say that at least a minor revolution has occurred in the general food industry as a secondary effect of Dave's invention.

Dave died in 1965, as mentioned, at the age of 80. Throughout his life he continued to have a consuming interest in new ideas and inventions. Truly they were an integral part of his life as well as ours. His contributions to society were varied and of unquestionable value.

In the opinion of J. L. Kraft, the cheese company founder, Dave Peebles "contributed more to the dairy industry than any other single man."

Alexander M. Poniatoff

Magnetic Tape Recorder

ALEX, AS HE WAS CALLED BY his friends, was one of the most interesting personalities I have known. He is well known for his long association with the Ampex Corporation, a major manufacturer of magnetic tape recorders and other products. First as President and then Chairman of the Board of Ampex for many years, he was in close contact with inventors who played a major role in developing Ampex products, including the well-known video tape recorder.

Alex was of Russian lineage, and had many of the characteristics that we normally associate with Russian men—tallness, a large frame, an impressive lean face, a bass voice and a perceptible accent. In general, he was a most impressive person.

A newspaper article appearing at the time of his death gives a good, but incomplete, account of his life and experiences before coming to the United States. An earlier newspaper article in the *Palo Alto Times* (October 4, 1957) gives a more complete account. At various times he told me about his war experiences and how he left Russia and became an American citizen.

Alex was a native of Kazan, Russia. He had an excellent technical education with degrees in electrical and mechanical engineering from the Imperial College in Moscow and then the Technical College of Karlsruhe, Germany.

Alex was completing his technical education at Karlsruhe in 1914 when the war broke out between Germany and France. Alex knew that it was essential for him to return to Russia immediately to avoid possible internment in Germany. After failing to cross the border at several places, he managed to make his way to the Belgian border in a boxcar of a freight train. Several other persons were in the car for the same purpose, including a friendly American who entertained Alex with stories

Alexander M. Poniatoff

181

PONIATOFF

about the virtues of San Francisco. Alex later said that the stories gave him an intense desire to see San Franciso someday. Many others at the border were also anxious to cross over into Belgium. An American lady, part of an American tourist group, noted that Alex did not have a traveling bag, which might have led the guards to hold him for questioning. She gave Alex one of her bags to carry, enabling him to proceed over the border into Belgium without questioning. Making good use of the language barrier, the lady managed to convince the guards that their entire group, including Alex, were Americans. Alex never had the opportunity to thank the lady or to obtain her name.

From Belgium Alex made his way to England with the intent to enlist in the British army, since it appeared that Germany had blocked all access to Russia. He was refused enlistment in the British army because he was unable to speak English. Since Alex was persistent in his desire to enlist, a group of nine Englishmen, presumably linguists capable of speaking Russian and English, undertook a crash program to teach him enough English to enlist. In five weeks, with all nine men in the act, he was taught basic English which he later found to be a great asset—although it did not get him into the British army. About the time the English teaching was completed Alex, being of draft age, received orders from the Russian Consulate in London to return to Russia by way of Newcastle, Scotland. Alex, with other Russian draftees, was then taken by ship via Norway or Sweden to Russia, and was inducted into the Russian Navy as an air pilot. Presumably Alex had qualified as an air pilot at an earlier date, or it is possible that again he was given a crash education program after he entered the Russian armed forces. He served as a pilot in the Russian Imperial Navy under Admiral Boris Doudenoff. Another one of the pilots was Alexander de Seversky, who later became well known in the United States for his work in aviation. During the war Alex's squadron was engaged in regular surveillance flights over the Bering Sea. Alex described his plane as quite primitive, with an open cockpit, which gave little protection in subzero weather.

During the Russian revolution (1917-1918) Alex, with other pilots, defected and joined the White Russian forces under Alexander

Kerensky. Kerensky had been Defense Secretary and then Premier of Russia during the confused period immediately preceding the success of the Bolshevik revolution. As the Bolsheviks began to take over, he organized the "white" military forces, presumably to prevent the revolution from spreading to all of Russia. The white forces were unsuccessful and were gradually forced to retreat until they finally reached the northeast part of Russia. About that time the commander of his squadron was killed, leaving Alex in command. The white forces became so decimated and disorganized that Alex lost all communication or direction from Kerensky. Alex then decided that the jig was up and he ordered the remainder of the squadron to fly into China, where they landed in Manchuria, probably at Shenuang (Mukden). Alex and the other pilots then reported to Admiral Kolchak, who was stationed near Harbin. This was a long walk since there was no other means of transportation. After listening to their story Kolchak realized that they might be charged with desertion by the Russian Navy. His solution was to give each of the pilots an honorable discharge. That meant they were no longer under the jurisdiction of the Russian military and could go anywhere they desired. Some of the pilots left with the intent of making their way back into Russia to their homes. However, Alex and one of the other pilots decided to proceed to Shanghai. They went to the nearest port hoping to find a ship that would take them to Shanghai. They had very little money between them, but they were fortunate in finding a fishing boat scheduled to go to Shanghai, and the skipper agreed to accept a relatively small fare for the trip. Having no connections and very little money, they lived on the beach of Shanghai for several days following their arrival. Eventually they were approached by a Russian resident who gave them quarters in an apartment that he owned. Alex volunteered to do electrical wiring for the Russian, which netted him some needed money. His knowledge of the English language was of great help in finding work in Shanghai. During the first year he was able to earn a living by translating Reuters press telegrams into Russian for a Shanghai newspaper. Later he secured a position with the Shanghai Power Company.

Alex remained in Shanghai until February 9, 1927. At that time he came to San Francisco on a ship named the *Korea Maru*, arriving March 4, 1927. After a short stay in San Francisco, during which he undoubtedly saw the sights of the city, he contacted the local General Electric office with a letter of introduction. They arranged a position for him in their research department in Schenectady, New York. After about five years with General Electric in Schenectady, he decided to return to San Franciso, because as he said, "I fell in love with San Francisco." General Electric had given him a letter of introduction to Pacific Gas and Electric Company in San Francisco. They gave him the assignment of mapping all the power lines in Napa County. He also designed automatic substations.

During the war period 1942-1944 Alex became a designer of electrical arc and vacuum furnaces and test equipment for steam turbines and axial flow compressors. This was at a plant in Sunnyvale, California which was reactivated during the war for the manufacture of engines and turbines for marine services. The president of that company was Charles Moore, who happened to be a very good friend of Tomlinson I. Moseley. Moseley was to organize the Dalmo Victor Company, where Alex was later hired as an engineer for the design of aircraft antennas.

In 1944 PG&E decided to reconsider their plans for expansion. At that time the leaders of many California corporations believed there would be somewhat of a depression following the war. In any event Alex again was looking for work. One of the companies he visited in search of a position was Wesix Company, manufacturers of electric air and water heaters. There he talked with Wesley Hicks, who was then president of the company. Hicks sent him to Tomlinson I. Moseley, who at that time had a manufacturing establishment making several products, including hair-waving equipment for beauty parlors. Moseley gave him the job of developing an improved electric heater for hair-waving machines. I first met Alex at Moseley's establishment. Alex was in a small room surrounded by wire, tools, and meters. When I was introduced to him he said very little and Moseley explained what he was doing. Alex did develop a better and safer hair-waving heater, which Moseley proceeded to manufacture. It was the first invention that he made while associated with Moseley, and is covered by U.S. Patent 2,152,359. Alex did other development work for Moseley, including an electric shaver which was never successfully commercialized. Later Moseley, together with Earl Douglas, organized the Dalmo Victor Company, and put Alex in charge of research and development. Alex remained with Dalmo Victor until after World War II.

The focus now shifts to a U.S. Army officer in the Signal Corps, Jack Mullin, who entered Germany near the end of the war with some of the first U.S. troops to cross the Rhine River. He had noted that Hitler's speeches over the radio were recorded and that the quality of reproduction was surprisingly good. He managed to find the place in Germany where the recorders were made, and was able to buy two machines and several reels of magnetic tape, all of which he shipped to San Francisco in a foot locker. These machines were known by the name of "Magnetophone." After leaving the Army he returned to San Francisco and proceeded to make some changes in the machines to improve their sound quality. The changes involved incorporating so-called high-frequency bias, which improved the quality of recording and reproduction. Then, together with W. A. Palmer, he established a sound studio in San Francisco (W. A. Palmer Films, Inc.), using the Magnetophone recorders. To further the use of the recorders, Mullin and Palmer contacted radio studios in Hollywood and interested Bing Crosby in giving the recorder a trial for radio broadcasting. With Mullin's assistance, some of Bing's programs were recorded and broadcast. Bing was delighted with the results, particularly because the recorder made possible editing by cutting out and adding portions of the tape. Bing asked Mullin and Palmer to sell him several machines for further use.

Since Mullin and Palmer did not have manufacturing facilities, they contacted Moseley at the Dalmo Victor Company, with the thought that Dalmo might be interested in engineering and manufacturing the recorders for Bing Crosby. Some time before, Moseley and Alex had formed a manufacturing firm by the name of Ampex Electric Company, which was a partnership of Alex and Moseley. They manufactured a special type of electric motor for aircraft radar. After the end of the war there was no further market for their product. Alex was interested in the Magnetophone recorder and witnessed one of the demonstrations in Los Angeles. However, Alex's interest was not shared by Moseley.

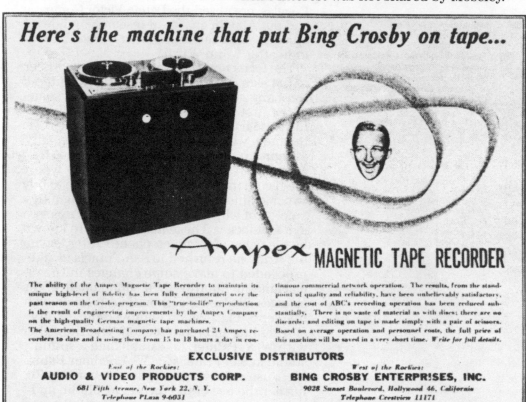

Here's the machine that put Bing Crosby on tape...

Ampex MAGNETIC TAPE RECORDER

The ability of the Ampex Magnetic Tape Recorder to maintain its unique high-level of fidelity has been fully demonstrated over the past season on the Crosby program. This "true-to-life" reproduction is the result of engineering improvements by the Ampex Company on the high-quality German magnetic tape machines.
The American Broadcasting Company has purchased 24 Ampex recorders to date and is using them from 15 to 18 hours a day in con-

tinuous commercial network operation. The results, from the standpoint of quality and reliability, have been unbelievably satisfactory, and the cost of ABC's recording operation has been reduced substantially. There is no waste of material as with discs; there are no discards; and editing on tape is made simply with a pair of scissors. Based on average operation and personnel costs, the full price of this machine will be saved in a very short time. *Write for full details.*

EXCLUSIVE DISTRIBUTORS

East of the Rockies:
AUDIO & VIDEO PRODUCTS CORP.
681 Fifth Avenue, New York 22, N. Y.
Telephone PLaza 9-6031

West of the Rockies:
BING CROSBY ENTERPRISES, INC.
9028 Sunset Boulevard, Hollywood 46, California
Telephone Crestview 11171

First advertisement for the Ampex Magnetic Tape Recorder (1948)

Since Crosby desired to purchase some of the machines, Moseley and Alex decided that Ampex Electric might take on the project provided that Crosby would submit a firm order for twenty machines, and in addition would make an advance payment of $2,000 for each machine. Crosby, who was represented by Boris Grillo in the negotiations, met these terms, which gave Ampex Electric sufficient capital to begin the manufacture of the machines. Later models of these machines became the Model 200 professional tape recorder that was subsequently manufactured by Ampex. As designed by Alex, the machine had all the desirable features of the Magnetophone, plus improvements, and was suitable for professional use by broadcasting stations.

The down payment received from Crosby proved to be insufficient to complete manufacture of the twenty machines. Ampex Electric contacted a local bank for a loan but without success, and then contacted Wells Fargo Bank in San Francisco. About the same time, a Philippine capitalist, Joseph McMicking, made known to Wells Fargo his desire to invest in some new electronic business. The bank introduced him to Moseley, with the thought that he might be interested in acquiring Ampex Electric. McMicking became interested in the tape recorder and also in Alex as an engineer. He agreed to purchase Moseley's interest and to finance completion of the recorder.

Ampex Audio Recorder used for commercial studio recording

After delivery of the recorders to Crosby, McMicking became even more interested and proceeded with incorporation of a company under the present name of Ampex Corporation. He made an agreement with Moseley for his interest, which probably included some cash payment and also a stock interest in the new corporation. A small building in Redwood City was provided by McMicking for the company, and McMicking, or the finance company that he represented, advanced capital for initial operations. Alex was made president of the new company.

Shortly before the deal with McMicking, I had occasion to visit Dalmo Victor and Moseley on another matter. When I arrived at the plant, the office was deserted but Alex happened to be in an adjacent part of the plant. After renewing our friendship, Alex referred to the recorder. He took me to a room where the recorder was installed with a loudspeaker for demonstration purposes. A short demonstration convinced me that the recorder was far better than anything I had ever heard.

The newly formed Ampex Corporation employed a group of young engineers in addition to Alex, including Walter Selsted, Harold Lindsey, and Myron Stolaroff, all of whom came from Dalmo Victor. The professional recorder, known as Model 200, found a profitable market for use in radio broadcasting, the motion-picture industry, and the record-making (phonograph records) industry. Many other recorders were added to the Ampex line, including high-precision commercial recorders, such as are used by the petroleum industry in making geophysical surveys.

Sometime before 1955, Walter Selsted and Alex became interested in the development of a magnetic tape machine for recording and reproducing video programs. As mentioned in another chapter, Radio Corporation of America (RCA) had demonstrated the possibility of recording video signals but their equipment was impractical for commercial use. Briefly, it used a standard magnetic tape driven at high speed past a magnetic recording head. Alex and Walter recognized the difficulties in developing a machine that would operate with a tape speed comparable to that of conventional voice recorders. Most audible voice frequencies are in the range of 200 to 15,000 cycles per second whereas video frequencies range up to 3.5 to 4 megacycles per second. They decided that one possibility was to use a wide magnetic tape and to record by repeatedly sweeping a magnetic head laterally across the tape. A search of the patent literature in the recorder field yielded an early U.S. patent (2,245,286) granted to an Italian inventor, which used this principle for sound recording.

Alex proposed that Ampex should start a new project for the development of a video recorder. Two men were selected to handle the project, namely, Charles P. Ginsburg and Ray

Dolby. Some months after the project began, I had occasion to visit Alex in February 1955. He said that Ginsburg and Dolby had set up some video-recording equipment that they might be able to demonstrate. We walked into that part of the plant, directly next to Alex's office, where Ginsburg and Dolby were working with their equipment.

As related in the chapter on Charles Ginsburg, the construction and operation of their breadboard model were explained to us at that time, and we witnessed the first demonstration.

The Ampex Magnetic Video Tape Recorder, which revolutionized the television industry

The chapter on Ginsburg also describes the great amount of further work required by the radio group to produce the first successful video tape recorder. Alex kept in close contact with the project and did not at any time doubt its eventual success. A number of private demonstrations were made by the research group as improvements were made. Each demonstration showed improvement in performance but also revealed further improvements that were required to produce

VTR

a machine that would be acceptable to the video broadcasting industry, and particularly to the networks where such a machine would have great value.

The Chicago demonstration to the video broadcasting industry, described by Charles Ginsburg, was an outstanding success. Before commercial sales could be made, however, it was necessary to package the machine. This required cooperation between the project group and production engineering. The first commercial sale was in 1956 to Columbia Broadcasting System (CBS) and was used for the first broadcast of recorded tape on November 30, 1956.

Late in 1956 Ampex officials had disturbing news about the development of a video tape recorder by RCA. Later, RCA openly approached Ampex about their development, and offered to demonstrate their machine to Ampex personnel. They explained that their machine recorded and reproduced in color, whereas the Ampex commercial machine would record and reproduce only in black and white. Color video at that time was not generally used by any of the broadcasting stations, although it was known that RCA had many patents covering color video systems, and that they wished to popularize color video in place of black and white.

As related in the chapter on Charles Ginsburg, Alex was involved in the decision to demonstrate that the Ampex black and white equipment, with minor changes, could be used for color recording and reproduction. He did not witness the RCA demonstration, but he received a detailed report from Ginsburg and the engineers that made the trip, and my report on the legal issues involved.

Shortly after the RCA demonstration, Alex and I met in New York City and I visited the patent department of RCA to obtain information concerning their thoughts on the matter. The RCA attorney to whom the matter had been delegated handed me a tentative agreement he had prepared. I returned to the hotel where we were staying and Alex and I went over their proposal. We noted a number of changes we thought advisable or essential. The proposed agreement and our suggestions were referred to Ampex officials and, after some further negotiation, it was executed by both parties.

Poniatoff (left) with Charles Ginsburg

The evening after our consideration of RCA's proposal, we decided to have dinner at a restaurant on Madison Avenue, several blocks south of our hotel (the Westbury). Shortly after arriving at the restaurant Alex discovered that his wallet was missing. He immediately concluded that it had been left at the hotel and that it would be advisable to go back to get it immediately, since it contained considerable cash. After a lapse of about one hour, he returned somewhat breathless, but with the wallet. He said that the wallet had not been in the hotel room, which led him to believe it might have been left at a small tea shop he had visited during the afternoon, to buy his special brand of tea. On his way back from the hotel he stopped at the tea shop and to his surprise it was still open. The shopkeeper had his wallet and was happy to see him. She had stayed open in the hope that he would return. Undoubtedly Alex had impressed her as being someone of importance!

About 1950 Alex felt he was sufficiently prosperous to undertake the building of a new home. He purchased a large lot in Atherton, California and retained a local architect whose work he had admired. Typical of Alex, he furnished the architect with detailed ideas and specifications for the new home. Eventually the architect produced blueprints which seemed to carry out Alex's ideas. The design was for a modern one-story house. Apparently Alex had some doubts about certain features of the plans, and he thought it best to submit the plans to another architect for criticism. Having long admired Frank Lloyd Wright, he decided to approach him for his professional advice and criticism. At that time Wright was living in Arizona, where his office and staff were located. One day Alex appeared at his office with his drawings and probably a letter of identification. When he explained his mission, Wright advised him that his staff was busy on large projects and that he could not be bothered with a small matter such as a house. He also explained that his fees were such that no individual could afford to contract for his services. As related by Alex, during the conversation he unrolled one of his blueprints and used it to explain to Wright what kind of advice he would like to have. This seemed to spark Wright's interest because he proceeded to look over the plans and give Alex the advice he wanted. Alex left on good terms with Wright and without paying anything for the interview.

After making revisions to the plans, Alex solicited bids from three contractors. He accepted the lowest bid, which proved to be a mistake. During the preliminary phases of building, he hired an inspector to make certain the contractor was properly following the plans. Shortly thereafter the contractor became bankrupt, which necessitated finding a new contractor to finish the job. Alex showed me the place shortly before it was completed. The ceiling was vaulted with lattice panels for good acoustics. The combined living and dining room was huge, about 40 feet wide and 50 feet long. At one end there was a circular-shaped, or what Alex termed a moon-shaped, fireplace. One inner wall was made to mount theater-type loudspeakers for his stereo sound system. The end wall, opposite the fireplace, was made of plywood panels set at angles to minimize echoes. The tiled concrete floor had several recessed areas to receive special rugs. The den had a picture window, at one end facing an oriental garden, which included a clump of birch trees to remind Alex of the birch forest that had surrounded his childhood home. A control panel mounted on one wall could be swung down to permit control of various electrical units, including the sound system. Thomas Church designed the layout for the surrounding grounds, including the parking area, patio, and garden. Planting of the garden areas continued over a period of many years.

Alex rarely mentioned religion in our conversations. However, on one occasion I mentioned the relationship between the Eastern Orthodox Church and the Episcopal Church in the United States. Alex expressed his regret that there was no Russian Orthodox Church in the Peninsula area. Some years later a small Russian Orthodox Church was established in Palo Alto. While he may not have been much of a churchgoer, he undoubtedly was pleased that the church existed and gave it his support.

My last conversation with Alex was about a year before his death. I made the engagement by phone with his secretary, who explained that we would have lunch in his office. Alex seemed to be his old self although he was using a walker and appeared to be crippled with arthritis. During our conversation he related his military experiences in Russia, including his participation with the white forces under Kerensky, his escape to the United States, and his early work in San Francisco. Additional information has been supplied by his wife, Hazel Hess Poniatoff, whom he married in 1932.

Aside from his technical interests, Alex had a lifelong interest in health—particularly the effect of diet on health. This interest may have been due to his contracting yellow fever while in Shanghai. In 1968 he founded the Foundation for Nutrition and Stress Research, which was later called the Bio-Research Institute. The Institute publishes a bulletin edited by Dr. Hans Weber, Associate Director.

Although Alex Poniatoff was not a prolific inventor, he worked continually with engineers engaged in research and development and they benefited from his encouragement and advice. When I spoke to his wife about his early work she explained that they were married after he came to live in California. However, she said that Alex spoke about his work at General Electric and that it resulted in six patents. What he probably told her was that he had submitted six disclosures of inventions to General Electric. His war-time work with Dalmo Victor was under government contract, with any inventions made there going to the government. His work in developing the tape recorder was certainly inventive but no patent applications were filed.

At the time of his death (October 24, 1980) a funeral service was held in the small Russian Orthodox Church in Palo Alto. The service was an unforgettable emotional experience for me and the others who attended. We filled the entrance and side wings of the cruciform interior; the casket was in a small central area. The service commenced after all were provided with lighted candles that we held for most of the service. The Russian choir sang intermittently with scriptural readings by the priest. It seemed to be a fitting finale for Alex.

Poniatoff (right) with Harold Lindsey at the introduction of the Ampex ATR-100

Walter T. Selsted

Tape Recorders and Consulting

ONE SELDOM FINDS AN engineer who is sufficiently versatile to serve as a valued consultant on diverse technical projects, as well as a corporate engineer and an inventor of sophisticated equipment. Walter Selsted fully has all these qualifications.

Selsted graduated from the University of California at Berkeley in 1946, with a Bachelor's degree in electrical engineering. His first engineering work (1946-1948) was to design and supervise construction of two radio broadcast stations, one in San Francisco and the other in Los Angeles. This work was for Pacific Broadcast Company, a broadcasting company located in San Francisco.

Before 1949 he was a consultant to Ampex Electric Company, and participated in their early decisions to enter into the magnetic recorder business. The original Ampex Electric Company was a partnership between Alexander Poniatoff and Tomlinson I. Moseley, which later became Ampex Corporation. By 1949 Ampex had redesigned the German Magnetophone recorder and had interested Bing Crosby in purchasing twenty of the machines. The redesigning is generally credited to Alex Poniatoff and became known as the Ampex Model 200. Selsted first served as a consultant to Ampex in connection with their decision to manufacture the Model 200 on a commercial basis. After incorporation under the name of Ampex Corporation, Selsted became a full-time employee.

As an employee of Ampex he was responsible for the design of many of the mechanical parts of their various magnetic tape recorders. In 1951 he became Chief Engineer, in 1955 Director of Research, and Corporate Vice President in charge of engineering in 1959. As Director of Research he was in constant close contact with all research projects, including the video tape recorder.

Walter T. Selsted

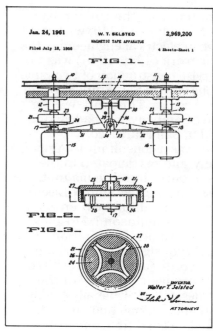

Jan. 24, 1961   W. T. SELSTED   2,969,200
                       MAGNETIC TAPE APPARATUS

Filed July 18, 1956   4 Sheets-Sheet 1

FIG_1_

FIG_2_
FIG_3_

INVENTOR
Walter T. Selsted

ATTORNEYS

*One of Selsted's many patents in the
field of tape recording*

While with Ampex he was one of the group of Ampex engineers who witnessed RCA's demonstration of their color video tape machine, on August 15, 1957, in Camden, New Jersey. After this demonstration he was one of the Ampex engineers invited to obtain more information about RCA's color video system. At that time, RCA employed about 100 research workers in a wide variety of projects. Selsted participated in discussions that followed in the Ampex organization concerning RCA's objectives, and probably was at least in part responsible for Ampex's cross-license agreement with RCA. More detail about these events is given in the chapters on Ginsburg and Poniatoff.

Aside from his work in directing various research projects, Selsted made many inventions and improvements to the various types of Ampex tape recorders. During this period (1949-1962), he is credited with some twenty-two U.S. patents in which he is named as inventor or co-inventor, all assigned to Ampex. A number of these patents related to technical fields other than tape recorders, including computer transports.

Selsted is nostalgic about his recollections of Alex Poniatoff. He recalls one of Alex's favorite expressions, namely that he wanted new recorders "to be as reliable as that big white box in the kitchen that makes cold."

After remaining with Ampex for about thirteen years, he resigned and accepted a position with the Hewlett-Packard Company in Palo Alto. While with Hewlett-Packard he served as Engineering Manager of their Mountain View Division. Much of his work was to design commercial equipment in the magnetic recorder field. He became acquainted with Dave Packard and Bill Hewlett and has a high regard for their capabilities and the unusual employee relations of their company.

Selsted continued to make inventions during his period with Hewlett-Packard. He is named as inventor or co-inventor in some five U.S. patents, all of which were assigned to Hewlett-Packard and relate mainly to magnetic tape transports and recorders.

After resigning from Hewlett-Packard he became a member of the Board and Chief Engineer of Data Measurements Corporation located in Mountain View, for the period 1969 to 1971. While with that company he participated in the design of tape recorder test instruments and computer terminals, and in their manufacture as commercial products.

Selsted resigned from Data Measurements in 1971, and became a professional technical consultant, specializing in the design of small machines and such projects as reduction of manufacturing costs, improvement of reliability, and failure analysis.

When asked about the extent of his activity as a consultant, Selsted named a surprising number of relatively large companies for which he has done research projects. Some of the larger companies were Radio Corporation of America, Hewlett-Packard, General Dynamics, Burroughs, Dictaphone, International Video, Castle & Cook's Arneson Products Division, Beckman Instruments' Spinco Division, and Eastman Kodak. In addition to his consulting work, he has also served as a technical expert in various legal actions, including particularly actions involving possible infringement of patents.

It is evident that Selsted has shown outstanding ability as an inventor, technical engineer, consultant, and technical expert. He is named as inventor in twenty-seven U.S. patents, most of which are in the magnetic tape recorder field.

Richard G. Sweet

High-Speed Jet Printer

THIS IS AN ACCOUNT OF AN invention that has become important to the printing and computer industries and has initiated significant developments in the medical field. It is one of a number of important inventions developed by research activities at Stanford University.

Richard G. Sweet graduated from the California Institute of Technology with the degree of Bachelor of Science in 1947. He was employed at the Applied Electronics Laboratory at Stanford from 1956 to 1966. It was the practice of that organization to submit various research proposals to the United States government for its consideration and approval. Approved projects were then funded by the government, with the research and development being carried out by the Applied Electronics Laboratory at Stanford.

Sweet became interested in high-speed printing, particularly for use in oscillographs. The direct-writing oscillographs available at that time did not successfully record frequencies in excess of about 200 cycles per second. He conceived the idea of controlling liquid ink droplets issuing from a jet nozzle, by applying signal-controlled electrical charges. Following customary procedure, he prepared and submitted a written proposal to the university organization handling research programs funded by the government. He described his ideas, proposing that the university might suggest such a program for funding by the government. The university submitted his project proposal to the Signal Corps of the U.S. Army which agreed to fund the research program. At that time contracts for such projects provided that the government would have a royalty-free nonexclusive license to any patent rights and that the inventor would retain title, provided he took on the responsibility for filing and prosecuting any patents that might be appropriate.

Richard G. Sweet

During the course of his initial work on the project, Sweet made an extensive literature search in the university's technical library. He learned from various publications that considerable experimental work had already been carried out on various methods for forming spaced liquid droplets in single file from a stream issuing from a pressure nozzle. His idea was to use ink as the liquid, and to control the droplets by electrical charges so that when the droplets were deposited on a sheet or a tape, markings would be printed indicating the manner in which electrical charging was controlled by a signal input. The oscillograph that he visualized would function to record high signal frequencies, of the order of 10,000 cycles per second or higher.

In his preliminary work he found that ink droplets could be electrically charged and that the amount of the charge could be varied according to a signal input. His first demonstrating apparatus applied signal charges to ink droplets as they were formed from an ink stream. Then the droplets were subjected to a constant electrostatic field whereby they were deflected laterally according to their signal charges. This apparatus operated quite well and demonstrated its ability to record frequencies well above 5,000 cycles per second.

With the consent of the university and the government, Sweet made a number of confidential demonstrations of his invention to engineers representing various firms that might be interested in proceeding with further development of commercial equipment. One firm contacted, Minneapolis Honeywell, was sufficiently interested to enter into an agreement in the form of an exclusive license except for the royalty-free rights of the government. Pursuant to the agreement, the Legal Department of Minneapolis Honeywell prepared and filed on July 31, 1963 an initial patent application in the U.S. Patent Office. Corresponding foreign applications were filed in six foreign countries.

Following the agreement with Minneapolis Honeywell, Sweet was not entirely satisfied with his first apparatus. He conceived a more elaborate apparatus that would be capable of drop-by-drop charging and interception of selected droplets. He developed new circuitry to make this type of droplet control possible, and this development greatly expanded the

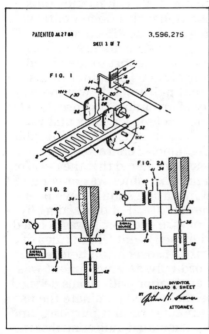

Drawings from Sweet's U.S. Patent 3,596,275, issued after the second application

possible commercial value of the invention. The further developments were reported to the university and to the Signal Corps, and also to Minneapolis Honeywell. Their Legal Department filed a second patent application March 25, 1964, disclosing and claiming his new ideas. The second application eventually claimed what was disclosed in both applications and the first application was later abandoned in favor of the second, the latter being then referred to as a continuation-in-part.

As required by the Signal Corps contract, Sweet prepared a comprehensive report, dated March 1964, entitled "High-Frequency Oscillography with Electrostatically Deflected Ink Jets," identified as Technical Report No. 1722-1, prepared under Signal Corps Contracts DA 36 (039) SC 87300 and DA 36 (039) AMC-03761 (E). The report, in printed booklet form, was submitted to the Signal Corps and copies were distributed to various government officials and departments, and also to non-government firms and organizations that were on the Systems Techniques Distribution List as of February 1964. In addition to describing Sweet's apparatus and method in detail, the report included a list of background literature and the names of all the parties on the distribution list.

Beginning in 1961 Sweet collaborated with R. C. Cumming in the development of an apparatus and method that made use of an array of jets, and which was disclosed and claimed in the Sweet-Cumming Patent 3,373,437. Sweet's later sales of his patent rights to A. B. Dick included his 50% interest in the Sweet-Cumming patent. In subsequent patent-infringement litigation this patent was held to be invalid because the improvement claimed was obvious as compared to the apparatus and method of the basic Sweet patent.

After filing and preparing the second application, Minneapolis Honeywell decided that they were not particularly interested in the project, and accordingly they voluntarily relinquished their exclusive rights and accepted a nonexclusive license. Under the new arrangement both applications were turned over to Sweet for prosecution. Sweet then arranged for me to take over prosecution in the United States and in foreign countries where applications had been filed.

Not long after I took over prosecution of the

pending applications, Sweet learned of a patent granted to another firm (Clevite), which appeared to disclose and claim part of Sweet's invention. One difference was that the patent disclosed and claimed the use of a matrix for graphic recording, such as the printing of letters and numerals. According to established procedure, certain claims of the issued patent were copied with minor changes into the Sweet application, and the Patent Office declared an interference for the purpose of determining whether Sweet or the other inventors were the first to invent and therefore entitled to the patent claims. The interference procedure involved submitting evidence in the form of exhibits and depositions on behalf of each party, followed by a final hearing before an Interference Examiner. Both parties took extensive depositions with documentary evidence bearing upon the effective dates of invention. The submitted evidence included a copy of Sweet's early report to the Signal Corps. The Interference Examiner in his decision held that neither side would be awarded priority of invention, because Sweet's disclosure did not include a matrix and was not specifically described as being applicable to printing alphanumeric characters.

Although it was considered that the decision of the Interference Examiner was unfair and that priority of invention should have been accorded to Sweet, instead of proceeding by way of appeal from the decision, it was decided to proceed under the Patent Office rules of practice by further prosecution before the Examiner. Accordingly, an amendment was filed in the last application with claims deemed to be of a scope that would dominate the use of Sweet's invention for various purposes, and an argument was submitted indicating that the case was in condition for allowance. Instead of proceeding with allowance of the application, the Examiner rejected claims on the basis of some literature references which disclosed experimental apparatus for forming liquid jets consisting of droplets in single file and which were for a purpose totally remote from recording by the use of ink droplets. These publications had been referred to in Sweet's early report to the Signal Corps and also in exhibits forming a part of the interference record. Upon amending the case by making some minor changes to the claims, and by

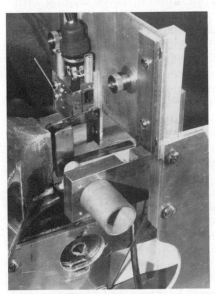

Some of Sweet's early apparatus

submitting an argument pointing out the differences between the referenced disclosures and the Sweet invention, the application was allowed.

Not long after the Sweet application issued as a patent, the A. B. Dick Company approached Sweet for purchasing his patent rights. After some negotiations Sweet agreed to an outright sale of his patent.

Since A. B. Dick acquired Sweet's patent rights, there has been substantial litigation in the federal courts charging infringement of the patent claims. The court decisions to date have differed somewhat. All decisions have sustained the patent as being valid, although there have been some differences with respect to the scope of the claims. Questions have been raised as to whether or not Sweet and his attorney should have disclosed to the Patent Office certain literature references that may not have been known to the Examiner until after the Sweet application was remanded to him for further prosecution, following the interference. These references included those disclosed to the Signal Corps in Sweet's early report and in the interference exhibits mentioned above. The Federal Court of Appeals finally held that these references should have been called to the Examiner's attention, even though they were disclosed in the infringement proceedings. Because of this the court held the patent to be unenforceable.

Following his work on the high-speed ink-jet invention, Sweet joined a group at Stanford that had obtained funding from the government for developing an apparatus and method to identify and sort biological cells. This project was based on work done by a group at the Los Alamos National Laboratory; they had demonstrated a cell sorter based in part on Sweet's droplet generation and deflection techniques. It was appreciated that such apparatus would be of tremendous value to the medical, biotechnical, pharmaceutical, and chemical industries. For example, it might be capable of identifying closely related types of biological cells at a relatively high rate, and also of isolating desired cells from a cell mixture. It was also appreciated that the relatively new genetic engineering technique produced a cell mixture and that one application of such a process could rapidly and efficiently separate the desired newly formed recombinant cells.

The project was successful in developing a new technique, which was described in the March 1976 *Scientific American*. The article was prepared by a group including Sweet and associated research workers Leonard A. Herzenberg and Lenore A. Herzenberg. Briefly, the method of operation involves tagging with a fluorescent dye certain cells in a mixture of different cells. Just before the droplets are formed, the jet stream is illuminated with the focused blue light of an argon-ion laser, which excites a yellow-green fluorescence in the tagged cells. The fluorescent light is detected along with laser light scattered from the cells, and the resulting electrical signals used to charge the liquid stream exactly when each droplet containing a desired cell is forming. Farther downstream the droplets that have retained their charge after they separate from the stream then pass through a constant electrical field across their path. This field serves to deflect the charged droplets toward a collecting reservoir, leaving the uncharged droplets to continue on their original course. As of this writing, such apparatus is being manufactured by several companies, including Becton Dickenson Electronics Laboratory in California, and it is anticipated that it will be widely used in the medical and pharmaceutical fields.

This story illustrates the efficacy of a knowledgeable technical engineer with a good idea, the excellent laboratory facilities of Stanford University, and persistence of the inventor in pursuing his patent rights. It also points up the value of government support for worthwhile research projects. Again it illustrates how a basic invention in one field can stimulate important inventions in other fields.

Albert R. Thompson

Food Processing Machinery

ALBERT R. THOMPSON WAS one of the most prolific and accomplished engineers and inventors in the west. He truly started from the bottom and ended at the top over a period of about fifty years. Most of his work was as an employee and officer of Food Machinery Corporation (FMC), one of the major U.S. companies that had its origins in the San Francisco Bay region.

The Thompson family migrated from England to the United States in the middle 1800's, and settled on a farm near Plainville, Illinois, where Al was raised and attended public school. The extent of his education is unknown but it is possible that he did not graduate from high school. It is known that before coming to California he worked in a bicycle shop in Chicago. The family migrated to California in 1901, and established their home in San Jose. In addition to the father, William Thompson, and the mother, Elizabeth Thompson, there were four children, Albert R. Thompson, Roy B. Thompson, Marion Thompson Kilpatrick, and Emma Thompson Bennett. Two additional children had died when young in Illinois.

One of the early predecessor companies of FMC was W. C. Anderson Horticultural Supplies, which manufactured a patented invention of Anderson's known as a "prune dipper." It was used to dip prune plums into caustic solution to prepare them for sun-drying.

In 1901 Anderson hired Albert Thompson, not as a mechanic, engineer or inventor, but as a janitor. According to one account, during his janitorial work in the machine shop, the mechanics were endeavoring to true some large spoked wheels. After observing that the mechanics were having difficulty, Thompson took over the job and very quickly had the wheels properly trued. Apparently Anderson became aware of what happened and shortly

Albert R. Thompson

205

thereafter promoted Thompson to work in the machine shop.

In 1902 the Anderson company merged with Barngrover Hull Company to form the Anderson Barngrover Company. Two years later they became active in the cannery equipment field with the manufacture of a so-called "syruper" which simultaneously filled twelve cans with syrup. In 1910 this company built a factory at 333 West San Jose Street in San Jose, California, which they occupied for twenty years. In 1928 Anderson Barngrover merged with an adjacent company, John Bean Spray Pump Company, to form Food Machinery Corporation (FMC). Due in part to the various activities of the merging companies, and to continued introduction of new products in the dairy and agricultural fields, the combined company commercialized a wide range of products that were either leased or sold in the United States and foreign countries.

Anderson Barngrover plant in San Jose, about 1920, with cars parked by hitching posts

One of the most outstanding and successful inventions made by Thompson was a completely automated cooker and cooler for the canning industry. The invention of a way to preserve food in sealed metal cans is attributed to Nicholas Appart, a Parisian confectioner. He cooked various foods in glass jars sealed with cork stoppers. It took some time after his pioneer work in 1810 for canning to be adopted by the food industry. Initially the seams and the ends of the metal cans were secured by solder. Later crimping was developed in place of solder and the inner surfaces were coated to reduce or eliminate the thickness of interior

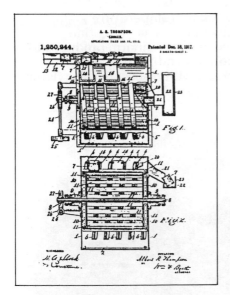

Thompson's first "Continuous Agitating Cooker," introduced in 1913, operated at atmospheric pressure and relatively low temperature

tin plating. Before 1910 it was common to cook and sterilize food after sealing by immersing the sealed cans in hot water maintained at a temperature of about 212° F for an extended period of time, depending upon the size of the cans and the nature of the food involved. This was a slow, costly process and one that was sometimes unreliable.

Thompson developed a cooker-cooler system that was completely automatic and employed steam in place of hot water. His first machine employed a steel cooker shell with slide valves for feeding the cans into and out of the closed ends of the shell. Within the shell the cans were progressed in a spiral or helicoidal path from the entrance to the discharge end. This mechanism was referred to as a "reel and spiral." The cans were continuously rolled as they progressed along the spiral path to the discharge end of the shells, producing continuous agitation of the contents with the result that they were heated more uniformly and in a shorter period of time. Upon leaving the cooker, the cans continued through a cooler where they were immersed in cold water. The first commercial cooker-cooler was introduced to the trade in 1913 and was an immediate commercial success.

The next improved cooker-cooler, also invented by Thompson, was introduced in 1915. It was equipped with so-called "pocket-type" valves, in place of the slide valves of the first cooker.

Thompson's third cooker-cooler was introduced to the trade in 1920. One of the principal improvements was the use of steam at a pressure above atmospheric, thus heating the cans to a temperature well above 212° F. Advantages were that the higher temperature insured effective sterilization, the cooking time was greatly reduced, a more uniform product was produced, and the product was of better quality, particularly with respect to color, flavor, and texture.

Thompson's third cooker-cooler

An immediate market for the third cooker was the evaporated milk industry, where it made possible the sterilization of milk to meet their critical requirements with respect to purity, color, flavor, and viscosity. For the particular needs of the milk industry, the sterilizing and cooling sections were constructed as a single unit, with one continuous cylindrical shell and direct progression of the cans from the sterilizer into the cooler. In the sterilizer section, the cans were heated in stages. The cooler was likewise operated under pressure to minimize differential pressure.

The impression that one might gain from the above is that Thompson made only three cooker inventions to protect the three commercial cookers that were introduced over the period of 1910 to 1920. However, in obtaining patent protection for such complicated equipment as an automatic pressure cooker, it is customary to secure patents covering features of the overall machine, and additional patents covering various component parts, such as special can-handling valves. During the years

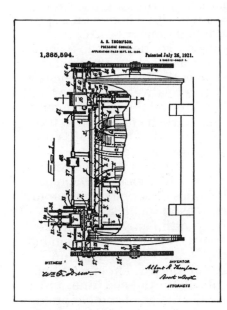

Drawing from patent for pressure cooker shown on previous page

following introduction of the 1920 pressure cooker, Thompson undoubtedly made many further improvements or modifications to make the pressure cooker suitable for customers with particular needs, and the commercial machines were continually improved. Such continuing development invariably calls for the creation of many secondary inventions.

From the beginning of his inventive career, Thompson did not confine his talents to pressure cookers in the canning industry. He was equally successful in inventing other equipment such as machines for pear peeling and fruit pitting, food freezers, and a variety of agricultural equipment, such as harvesters for various crops. Over nearly fifty years with FMC, Thompson is credited with some 200 U.S. patents.

In many instances prolific inventors do not develop administrative skill and business judgment, but this was not the case with Thompson. Over the many years of his employment by FMC, he became a vice president in charge of engineering, a member of the corporate Board of Directors, and a member of the Executive Committee, an unusual record of accomplishment for one lacking in a college education and starting as a bicycle repairman and a janitor.

During a recent discussion with Albert Thompson's son, Stewart Thompson, he spoke highly of his father as a great family man. Even with all his work for FMC, he managed to maintain good communications and relations with his wife and children, and to avoid family conflicts. Stewart mentioned that it was not unusual for his father to review design problems after retiring at night and he vividly recalls some times hearing his father exclaim, "I've got it!"

About 1945, one of Thompson's inventions pertaining to a pear-peeling machine was involved in an interference proceeding in the U.S. Patent Office, with an application filed by another party (Dunn) and assigned to Del Monte Corporation. I was retained by FMC to represent them. An interference proceeding in the U.S. Patent Office is for the purpose of determining priority of invention, when two applicants are claiming the same inventive subject matter. The invention was an improved pear peeler equipped with a special feeding means which, upon receiving a pear, would carry out general alignment of the pear before it was introduced into the main part of the machine. Both parties presented evidence with respect to their dates of invention, including documents such as drawings and descriptions, and the depositions of the inventors and witnesses. Working with Thompson in preparing for his deposition was a pleasure. Possibly from prior experiences, he readily understood what was involved and the type of evidence required. His first drawing showing the invention was a relatively good free-hand sketch that illustrated all the essential parts of the improvement. He had referred to this sketch in his presentation to an FMC committee which made decisions on appropriations for development of new ideas. An engineer was designated to work with Thompson to prepare engineering drawings of a commercial prototype. For some reason the design that Thompson directed the engineer to make was not the same as the design shown in his original sketch. Before the engineering drawings were completed, Thompson had second thoughts about the machine, and decided to begin the design of another prototype, adhering more closely to his original ideas. Thus, engineering drawings were prepared for two different prototypes. Patent applications were prepared and filed on both embodiments, but the interference involved only the first application. Dunn's history of development was open to criticism in that he did not build and test a prototype until after he had proven the operativeness and value of a special so-called "profile cutter" that he was advocating. The first decision by the interference board was in favor of Dunn on the grounds that the delay in building a prototype was a prudent thing to do rather than immediately building the prototype with the special cutter. However, on appeal to the Court of Customs and Patent Appeals, the decision was reversed in favor of Thompson. Unfortunately Thompson died on September 19, 1947, before the Federal Court's decision.

Albert Thompson is an example of a highly motivated and successful inventor who succeeded in spite of a lack of what we would now consider to be a necessary technical education.

Russell H. Varian

Klystron Tube

RUSSELL H. VARIAN (RUSS) IS well known for the invention of the Klystron tube, a type of vacuum tube widely used in the electronic industry.

A book entitled *The Inventor and the Pilot,* authored by Russell Varian's widow Dorothy, deals with the lives of both Russell and his brother Sigurd (Sig), their inventions, the organization of Varian Associates, Inc., and the early growth of the corporation. The book, published in 1983 by Pacific Books, of Palo Alto, California, is highly recommended as a thorough and interesting history of the Varian brothers and their activities as inventors.

This account is primarily concerned with Russell Varian, his inventions, including particularly the Klystron tube, and various experiences I had with Russell and Varian Associates over a period from about the fall of 1951 to the summer of 1953. During a later period, when I represented Felix Bloch in his licensing of nuclear magnetic resonance (NMR), I again had frequent contacts with Russ and other members of the company.

Dr. Bloch executed his first exclusive license agreement with Russell Varian as of September 30, 1948. This initial license was superseded by a second agreement dated October 1, 1953. Some months before execution of the second agreement, Paul Hunter, one of the original Varian Associates, who had been employed by Sperry Gyroscope in their legal department, came to California and assumed a position with the company as a director and head of its Legal Patent Department.

My work as patent counsel for Varian Associates was for a relatively short period. Some time after Paul Hunter began his position with Varian, Felix Bloch requested that I represent him on contract matters. With the consent of Varian Associates, I undertook to represent Dr. Bloch on various matters, including licensing negotiations between

Russell H. Varian

Varian and various sublicensees, and monitoring accounting for the royalties paid by licensees on NMR equipment. This brought me into frequent contact with Russell Varian and other officials of Varian Associates.

In the early days of radio, various types of equipment were used for the generation of electromagnetic waves. Wavelengths on the order of 200 to 600 meters were widely used for commercial ship-to-shore communication. A popular type of ship-to-shore equipment employed a rotary alternating current generator having a 500-cycle output, which was connected to a high-voltage transformer in series with an operating key. The secondary of the transformer, which might have an output on the order of 5,000 to 20,000 volts, was connected in a circuit including a capacitance, a form of spark gap, and the primary coil of an inductance coupler. The secondary of the coupler was connected to ground and to the antenna. This type of equipment was highly inefficient, particularly since a spark gap is an inefficient generator of electromagnetic waves. The more elaborate and expensive Poulsen arc transmitter, commercialized to some extent by Federal Telegraph, was subject to operational difficulties and also lacked efficiency. A relatively few high-power commercial radio stations made use of large rotary generators constructed to produce an output of long wavelength (e.g., 10,000 to 20,000 meters) directly coupled to the antenna. Such generators were efficient but costly to construct.

The original laboratory experimental equipment constructed by Hertz in the nineteenth century produced relatively short high-frequency electromagnetic waves. Hertz demonstrated that such waves could be focused as a beam. His transmitting equipment used what is commonly known as a spark coil operating from batteries, with the output of the spark coil connected to a spark gap and an antenna loop. The waves were detected by another loop having its ends separated by a short gap, so that reception of the transmitted waves was detected by visible sparks across the gap.

The first "wireless" equipment produced and demonstrated by the Marconi Company early in this century made use of the coherer as a detector. Subsequently Marconi employed the two-element vacuum tube invented by Fleming. Crystal detectors were also widely used in place of vacuum tubes. They made use of natural crystals such as ferrites and galena. The galena "cat whisker" detector was widely used by amateurs and for simple sets used to receive broadcast programs. Later some amateurs employed the three-element vacuum tubes but, as supplied by de Forest, they were too erratic for extensive commercial use.

All the early radio systems were highly susceptible to static electricity. During the summer months radio telegraph signals and radio programs were practically obliterated by receiver noise or static produced by continual electrical discharges in the atmosphere. Long wavelength signals were also susceptible to such static, although to a lesser degree.

At an early date Russell and Sig Varian became interested in developing a reliable guidance system for aircraft. Sig at that time was a Pan American pilot on flights in Mexico and Central America. He became aware of the critical need for reliable guidance systems for aircraft and for spotting planes under conditions of poor visibility. As the brothers studied the problem it became apparent that a practical and reliable system would require equipment which would produce a coherent electromagnetic wave beam that would reflect when directed toward a metal body (e.g., the body of an aircraft), and for the reflected waves to be detectable as received at the source of the beam. They decided that these requirements called for the use of relatively short waves in the microwave range (e.g., 3-12 cm). Their sources of information indicated that no existing microwave generator would satisfy these requirements. This led them to undertake development of apparatus that would generate microwave energy of sufficient power to make possible a reliable and practical guidance system.

Preliminary work culminated in the first conception of the Klystron tube as evidenced by Russell's well-publicized sketch dated July 21, 1937. It employed the so-called "bunching" or velocity modulation feature, together with the cavity resonator feature that had been invented by William Hansen and was known as the "Rhumbatron." (The name "Klystron" was coined from a Greek word related to the "bunching" concept.) Hansen at that time

Russell Varian's famous sketch of the Klystron tube (July 21, 1937)

Russell and Sig (standing) with an early Klystron

was an associate professor in the Physics Department of Stanford University and a research worker with Sig and Russell. Russell had made arrangements to use a part of the Stanford physics research laboratory to develop his concept. Hansen was interested in the project and his frequent advice was a valuable asset, particularly on such matters as the feasibility of Russell's ideas.

Russell showed his sketch and related work to Hansen for his reaction. After careful consideration Hansen's reaction was definitely favorable. He urged Russell to proceed with the construction and testing of such a device.

The next step, making a prototype, was delegated to Sig, because of his talent for constructing intricate precision models. The model Sig produced was made of carefully machined metal parts. For testing to determine whether or not the device was generating microwaves, a velocity spectrograph screen was prepared which would fluoresce when bombarded with electron energy. The test of the first model produced only a few flashes but they were enough to convince Russell that he was on the right track. The second model was prepared with some improvements and when tested the results were somewhat better but still unsatisfactory. A third model was then prepared, with further improvements. When tested, it worked remarkably well and brightly lighted the screen. A crystal detector and tuned circuit were used with a galvanometer to determine the wavelength, which proved to be 13 cm. It was evident that the model was functioning with a substantial output, since the electromagnetic waves could be picked up in all parts of the room.

The first successful test of an invention to prove its utility is an important event, which in this instance took place on August 30, 1937. Usually it is an emotional event for the inventor, who suddenly realizes that he has created something of importance to the world.

About the time that the research program to develop the Klystron was started, agreements were made between the Varians and Stanford University, and between Stanford University and Sperry Gyroscope. The agreements called for a limited amount of financing by both Sperry and Stanford, to defray expenses of the research activity. Sperry was to have an exclusive license, under patent rights that might be obtained, to manufacture and sell the products resulting from the research. Royalty to be paid by Sperry was to be divided between Stanford and the Varian brothers. Under the terms of this agreement, Sperry was to be kept advised of the results of the research program, and particularly of the development of the first successful Klystrons. Sperry also engaged in a research program of its own to develop similar products for commercial manufacture and sale.

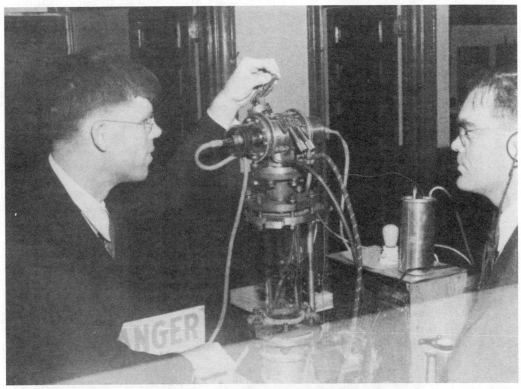

Russell Varian (left) and William Hansen working on a Klystron at Stanford University

When an inventor makes a basic invention having broad application he is sometimes tempted to encourage wide publicity. Russell appreciated the risk involved in premature publicity before exploring all the various fields of application, each of which would require additional inventions. In subsequent research carried on at Stanford by Russell, Bill Hansen, and Sig Varian, these fields of application were explored and further inventions made for which patent applications were filed. For example, Russell, Hansen, and Sig discovered that with certain changes the Klystron would serve as a detector of microwaves, an amplifier, or a combined generator and detector.

One of the first applications explored was a detection system for aircraft (now known as radar), which had been one of Russell and Sig's original research objectives long before the Klystron was developed. Equipment was assembled, including a Klystron microwave generator with parallel mirrors arranged to project a microwave beam. An object was placed at considerable distance from the generator to simulate an aircraft. It was found that the beamed microwaves were effectively reflected back to the source, thus providing a system usable for the detection of aircraft. It was known that a receiver could be made which would determine the phase between two closely spaced signals from the source, thus indicating the distance of the object from the source of the beam.

The Stanford laboratory where Klystron development took place

During World War II Klystrons were classified equipment supplied only to the military, and thus no commercial sales were made. The British military was supplied with classified technical data, enabling them to construct tubes suitable for airborne radar. Some of the early Klystron generators developed by the British were used effectively to spot German planes. Without such equipment the war might have ended differently.

Clockwise from lower left: Russell and Sigurd Varian, David Webster, William Hansen, and John Woodyard with early Klystron

Russell's widow Dorothy characterizes him as having a wide variety of interests beyond science and technology. One experience that I had not only confirmed her characterization but also demonstrated his tenacity in pursuing a train of thought. During the period of my legal services for the company I accompanied Russell and several others, including Myrl Stern and probably Sig, on a one-day trip to Los Angeles, leaving by air in the morning and returning in the late afternoon. The purpose was to negotiate a license agreement for use of NMR in a new technical field. The negotiations went well so we decided to return to the airport earlier than planned. We arrived at the airport more than one hour ahead of our scheduled departure so we walked over to the restaurant and bar which was then located a short distance from the terminal building.

After beginning on the first round of drinks, Russ started to talk about some of his views of social patterns in our society. The subject was interesting and developed much cross talk. During the second round of drinks someone announced with some concern that we had missed our flight. We returned to the airport and were able to book on a later flight without much of a wait. As we entered the DC-6 Russ, who was first, headed for the lounge room and table in the tail end of the ship. There Russ immediately continued the discussion on the same subject. By the time we arrived in San Francisco Russ was explaining his idea that cultural behavior not only followed certain set patterns, but that he could derive mathematical formulas which would make it possible to forecast behavior under certain circumstances.

Russell had become acquainted with Felix Bloch as early as 1933. Probably he first learned about the successful operation of the NMR equipment in 1946. However, I recall that in one conversation with me, Russ said he attended a meeting of a technical group at which Dr. Bloch explained the laboratory work by Bill Hansen and himself in constructing and operating the first NMR equipment. Mrs. Varian believes that Russ did not attend such a meeting but was told about the NMR research by someone who was there. Russ told me that after learning about the NMR work he talked to Bloch and suggested that the equipment could be developed into a valuable commercial

James W. Geriak of Lyon and Lyon. Although Judge Renfrew had not previously tried a patent case, he readily understood the issues involved. It was stipulated that the trial would first try the issues of patent validity, scope of the patent, patent abuse and anti-trust violation, and thereafter the issue of infringement of the patent and damages. The last two issues were to be tried only if the patent were to be held valid in the first proceedings.

At the termination of the trial on the first issues, the patent was held to be valid. However, the claims of the patent were held to be limited in scope to use of fabric impregnated and dried at the mill to leave a moisture content of from 2 to 8% and to provide only uncured resin in the fabric as supplied to the garment manufacturer. Koratron was held to be guilty of patent abuse and in violation of Section 2 of the Sherman Anti-Trust Act.

The anti-trust violation involved a series of events between Koratron, an eastern mill (Dan River), and a small garment manufacturer in Los Angeles. Before the filing of legal action by Levi Strauss, Koratron filed a court action against another garment manufacturer in Los Angeles for patent infringement. Since the garment manufacturer had been using resin-impregnated fabric made by the eastern mill, it notified the mill with the expectation that the mill would take care of the matter. The mill then sent a representative to Koratron and demanded that Koratron dismiss its action against the manufacturer and agree that the mill could continue the sale of its fabrics without being charged with infringement. Koratron agreed with this arrangement but instead of simply dismissing the action against the manufacturer, it induced the manufacturer to sign a consent decree holding the patent valid and infringed. In subsequent publicity, Koratron made reference to the consent decree, creating the impression that its patent position had been strengthened.

The decision of Judge Renfrew was favorable to the defendants, since the limitation placed on the patent claims meant that the patent did not claim the process actually being used by the defendants. It was suggested that the parties should negotiate for the purpose of settling the litigation. Eventually a settlement was arranged, which absolved all the parties of any possible future charges or damages.

Koratron made no further attempts to litigate its patent rights, although it was subsequently sued by a garment manufacturer in an effort to collect damages for anti-trust violation. The plaintiff in that instance was not successful.

Although this is not the story of a successful, hard-working inventor, several things make it interesting. The first circumstance was that the inventors did not share in the collected royalty of twenty million dollars, since they had assigned their rights to Koret for a nominal consideration. Koratron, in its desire to gain the utmost amount in royalties, adopted the illegal tie-in system of the fabric mill and garment manufacturer. Koratron did not succeed in covering up the Dan River matter, and made matters worse by inducing the garment manufacturer involved to take a consent decree holding the patent valid and infringed, and then publicizing the decree in an effort to bolster the patent.

The moral of the story is obvious.

Index of Names

Photo Credits

1 (Bloch)—Mrs. Felix Bloch, **(Hansen)**—Varian Associates; **3**—Mrs. Felix Bloch; **4**—Varian Associates; **7, 8, 9, 10**—Mrs. Felix Bloch; **11**—(unknown); **13**—Merck & Company, Inc.; **23, 24, 25, 26, 27**—Marcus Lothrop; **31**—Ray Dolby/Dolby Laboratories, Inc.; **33**—Oakland Tribune, Feb. 28, 1988; **37**—Ray Dolby/Dolby Laboratories, Inc.; **42**—San Francisco Chronicle, April 10, 1989; **45**—(unknown); **46, 47 (de Forest), 48, 49, 50**—"The Tall Tree", May, 1958; **55, 61, 64**—René Gaubert; **67**—(unknown); **72, 74, 77, 78**—Charles P. Ginsburg/Ampex Corporation; **79, 93**—Marvin M. Grove; **97, 98, 99, 100, 102**—Hewlett-Packard. **105**—San Mateo Times, Feb. 2, 1987; **109, 113**—Barbara Hicks Moskowitz; **121**—"The Tall Tree," May, 1958; **122**—"Forty Years of Radio Research," George C. Southworth, 1962; **123**—Scientific Paper of the Bureau of Standards, No. 235; **124, 130**—Scientific Paper of the Bureau of Standards, No. 428; **139, 143, 144, 146, 148, 156**—The Merrill Company; **159, 162, 164**—The Rockwell Manufacturing Company; **167**—Leo H. Francis; **181, 186, 187, 189**—Ampex Corporation; **190, 191**—Hazel A. Poniatoff; **193**—Ampex Corporation; **195**—Walter T. Selsted; **199, 203**—Richard G. Sweet; **205, 296, 207, 208**—Stewart Thompson/FMC Corporation; **211, 213, 214, 215, 216, 217, 218**—Varian Associates.